THE ULTIMATE
PITTSBURGH PENGUINS
TRIVIA BOOK

A Collection of Amazing Trivia Quizzes
and Fun Facts for Die-Hard Penguins Fans!

Ray Walker

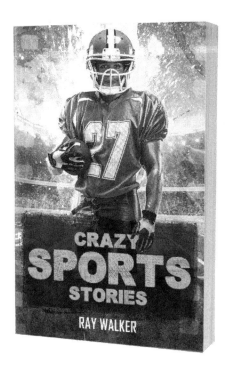

CONTENTS

INTRODUCTION

Team fandom should be inspirational. Our attachment to our favorite teams should fill us with pride, excitement, loyalty, and a sense of fulfillment in knowing that we are part of a community with many others who feel the same way.

Pittsburgh Penguins fans are no exception. With a rich, successful history in the NHL, the Penguins have inspired their supporters to strive for greatness with their tradition of colorful players, memorable eras, big moves, and unique moments.

This book is meant to be a celebration of those moments, as well as an examination of the collection of interesting, impressive, and important details that allow us to understand the full stories behind the players and the team.

You may use the book as you wish. Each chapter contains twenty quiz questions in a mixture of multiple choice, true or false formats, an answer key (Don't worry, it's on a separate page!), and a section of ten "Did You Know" factoids about the team.

Some readers will use this book to test themselves with the quiz questions. How much Penguins history did you know? How many of the finer points can you remember?

Some will use it competitively (Isn't that the heart of sports?), waging contests with friends and fellow devotees to see who can lay claim to being the biggest fan.

Some will enjoy it as a learning experience, gaining insight to enrich their fandom, and add color to their understanding of their favorite team.

Still, others may use it to teach, sharing the wonderful anecdotes inside to inspire a new generation of fans to hop aboard the Penguins bandwagon.

Whatever your purpose may be, we hope you enjoy delving into the amazing background of Pittsburgh Penguins hockey!

Oh…and for the record, information and statistics in this book are current up to the beginning of 2020. The Penguins will surely topple more records and win more awards as the seasons pass, so keep this in mind when you're watching the next game with your friends, and someone starts a conversation with "Did you know…?".

CHAPTER 1:

ORIGINS & HISTORY

QUIZ TIME!

1. In which year did the Penguins begin playing in the National Hockey League?

    a. 1957

    b. 1967

    c. 1977

    d. 1981

2. For over forty years, the Penguins played their home games in an arena that did not feature a sponsor appearing in the name (Civic Arena).

    a. True

    b. False

3. When the NHL accepted Pittsburgh into the league, how much money was their ownership group required to pay?

    a. $500,000 entry fee and $20,000 start-up costs

    b. $2,500,000 entry fee and $750,000 start-up costs

    c. $5,000,000 entry fee and $2,000,000 start-up costs

    d. $9,000,000 entry fee and $5,000,000 start-up costs

4. In which season did the Penguins begin to play in their new arena (Consol Energy Center – later renamed PPG Paints Arena)?

    a. 2005-06
    b. 2008-09
    c. 2010-11
    d. 2015-16

5. The Penguins' official website features pictures of its 16 greatest players, collected as their "All-Time Team." Only one of these players is pictured wearing a mustache; which one?

    a. Pierre Larouche
    b. Les Binkley
    c. Syl Apps
    d. Rick Kehoe

6. In which season did the Penguins earn their first-ever playoff berth and achieve their first-ever playoff series win?

    a. 1968
    b. 1970
    c. 1974
    d. 1976

7. The Penguins were the first team formed in their expansion class to defeat one of the "Original Six" NHL teams.

    a. True
    b. False

8. How many times in their franchise history have the Penguins won a division title?

    a. 0
    b. 3
    c. 6
    d. 8

9. Who was the first Penguin ever to be named as Pittsburgh's representative in the NHL All-Star Game?

    a. Ken Schinkel
    b. Les Binkley
    c. Leo Boivin
    d. Lou Angotti

10. Where do the Pittsburgh Penguins rank among NHL franchises when it comes to most Stanley Cup championships won?

    a. 2nd
    b. 7th
    c. 10th
    d. 15th

11. How did the Penguins fare during their 50th anniversary season in the NHL?

    a. Missed the playoffs
    b. Lost in the 1st round
    c. Lost in the Finals
    d. Won the Stanley Cup

12. Pittsburgh had the worst record in the league in both 1983 and 1984, which led to speculation that they once again might fold or be relocated to another city.

    a. True
    b. False

13. The Pittsburgh Penguins radio network, WXDX-FM, broadcasts across a Penguins home area that includes which four states?

    a. Pennsylvania, West Virginia, Virginia, and North Carolina
    b. Pennsylvania, West Virginia, Ohio, and Maryland
    c. Pennsylvania, New York, New Jersey, and Delaware
    d. Pennsylvania, New York, Ohio, and Michigan

14. Pittsburgh's current top farm team plays in the American Hockey League. What is this team called?

    a. Charlotte Checkers
    b. Cleveland Monsters
    c. Wilkes-Barre / Scranton Penguins
    d. Hershey Penguins

15. In 2012 and 2013, star center duo Sidney Crosby and Evgeni Malkin signed long-term contracts to remain with the Penguins for many seasons. How long were those contracts, respectively?

    a. 12 years and 8 years
    b. 10 years and 7 years
    c. 15 years and 10 years
    d. 8 years and 6 years

16. Pittsburgh has sent more players to the Winter Olympics to represent their countries than any other NHL franchise.

    a. True
    b. False

17. In the 2000s, which team did Pittsburgh face in back-to-back Stanley Cup Finals (with each team winning once)?

    a. Colorado Avalanche
    b. Detroit Red Wings
    c. Dallas Stars
    d. Chicago Blackhawks

18. The Penguins players made history after winning the 1991 Stanley Cup by doing what?

    a. Starting the popular trend of yelling the famous phrase "I'm going to Disney World!" into the television cameras
    b. Becoming the first NHL team to have customized commemorative Stanley Cup championship rings produced
    c. Becoming the first NHL team to visit the American president (George H.W. Bush) in the White House
    d. Flying to Jamaica for a week-long team celebration at a five-star beachfront resort

19. What is the name of the Pittsburgh Penguins mascot?

    a. Pingu
    b. Mr. Freeze
    c. Captain Waddles
    d. Iceburgh

20. The Pittsburgh Penguins were the first expansion franchise to win a Stanley Cup.

    a. True

    b. False

QUIZ ANSWERS

1. B – 1967

2. A – True

3. B – $2,500,000 entry fee and $750,000 start-up costs

4. C – 2010-11

5. D – Rick Kehoe

6. B – 1970

7. A – True

8. D – 8

9. A – Ken Schinkel

10. B – 7th

11. D – Won the Stanley Cup

12. A – True

13. B – Pennsylvania, West Virginia, Ohio, and Maryland

14. C – Wilkes-Barre / Scranton Penguins

15. A – 12 years and 8 years

16. B – False

17. B – Detroit Red Wings

18. C – Becoming the first NHL team to visit the American president (George H.W. Bush) in the White House

19. D – Iceburgh

20. B – False

DID YOU KNOW?

1. Pittsburgh has played in six different divisions as the NHL has undergone realignment through the years. The Penguins have been in the West, Norris, Patrick, Northeast, Atlantic, and Metropolitan divisions. They have also been part of the Prince of Wales Conference and the Eastern Conference.

2. Many years before the Penguins were added to the league, there had been a short-lived NHL franchise in Pittsburgh known as the Pirates. They played from 1925-1930 before moving to Philadelphia.

3. In 1975, the Penguins filed for bankruptcy after creditors called in some loans, and it appeared that the franchise might fold or be moved to Seattle. However, much to the relief of fans, shopping mall tycoon Edward J. DeBartolo Sr. purchased the team and decided to keep it in Pittsburgh.

4. The AHL's Pittsburgh Hornets were a relatively successful AHL team that won the Calder Cup in 1967. However, they folded permanently after that championship season, as the Penguins opened up in the NHL, and the local market could not support both clubs. The Penguins were required to pay a fee to the Detroit Red Wings, who had owned and operated the Hornets.

5. Led by superstar Mario Lemieux, the mid-1980s' Penguins narrowly missed the playoffs for three years in a row

(twice agonizingly falling short by just one game on the final day of the season), before breaking through in 1989 with a 2nd place finish in the Patrick Division and a playoff series victory over the New York Rangers in the 1st round.

6. After numerous financial difficulties bankruptcies, and threats of relocation, in 2007, Penguins ownership announced the creation of a new arena and a 30-year lease at that arena, keeping the team in Pittsburgh and finally allowing fans to relax about the future of the franchise.

7. Pittsburgh's biggest NHL rival is generally thought to be the Philadelphia Flyers, as both teams play in the same division and are in close geographic proximity. The Flyers have the advantage in the head-to-head rivalry, but the Penguins have won more championships.

8. The Penguins have cycled through many broadcasters over their years in the NHL. Three consecutive times they hired former players as color commentators: Peter Taglianetti lasted just one season. He was replaced by Ed Olczyk, who left after four years to become Pittsburgh's head coach. He was followed by Bob Errey, who found more success and lasted over a decade.

9. A surprising rivalry exists between Pittsburgh and the Washington Capitals. The rivalry was created mainly through playoff matchups, with the two teams meeting in eleven playoff series. The Penguins have dominated with nine wins in those series; although, they did lose to the Capitals when the rivalry was featured in the outdoor Winter Classic in 2011 at Heinz Field.

10. In the beginning, the Penguins went seven seasons without posting a winning record, before recording a 37-28-15 mark in 1974-75. They later went eight consecutive seasons without a winning record, before halting the skid in 1987-88.

CHAPTER 2:

JERSEYS & NUMBERS

QUIZ TIME!

1. When they began playing in the NHL, the Penguins used what color scheme for their uniforms?

   a. Black, gold, and white
   b. Black and white
   c. Dark blue, light blue, and white
   d. Red, yellow, and orange

2. The Penguins first added player names to the back of their jerseys after Mario Lemieux was drafted in 1984, to capitalize on his wild popularity with fans and sell more merchandise.

   a. True
   b. False

3. Michel Briere played only 86 games with the Penguins franchise, yet Pittsburgh has retired his jersey number, 21. Why?

   a. He scored six game-winning goals during the playoffs

for them, including the clincher for their first Stanley Cup win.

    b. He remained active in the community for decades after leaving the team, and contributed heavily to many philanthropic endeavors.

    c. Owner Jack Riley believed that the rafters in Civic Arena looked too empty compared to other NHL homes, and wanted to get a banner up as soon as he could.

    d. He passed away as a result of a car crash after finishing second in rookie of the year voting for the Penguins.

4. Which major sports team lodged an official protest with the NHL when Pittsburgh proposed its color change in 1980?

    a. Toronto Maple Leafs

    b. Boston Bruins

    c. Buffalo Sabres

    d. Pittsburgh Pirates

5. Aside from the usual Penguin logo, what else have the Penguins frequently sported on the front of their jerseys?

    a. The popular city nickname "Steeltown" written in yellow script with a silver underline

    b. A picture of an igloo superimposed over the shape of the state of Pennsylvania

    c. The initials "PP" written in large yellow block letters, simultaneously signifying both "Pittsburgh Penguins" and "Pittsburgh, Pennsylvania"

   d. The word "Pittsburgh" written diagonally across the chest

6. Which jersey number has proven to be most popular with Penguins, having been worn by 34 players?

   a. 9
   b. 11
   c. 23
   d. 31

7. For the first Penguins game after Mario Lemieux was forced to retire, the team asked for and received special permission from the NHL for all of their players to wear number 66 in tribute.

   a. True
   b. False

8. Who is the player to wear the highest-numbered jersey in Penguins franchise history?

   a. Petr Nedved
   b. Aleksey Morozov
   c. Sidney Crosby
   d. Rick Tocchet

9. Why did star center Sidney Crosby choose to wear number 87 on his jersey?

   a. It represents the number of goals he would ideally like to score in a season.
   b. It was his beloved grandfather's age at the time of his passing, just after Crosby had been drafted into the NHL but before he had played a game.

c. He was born on August 7, 1987.

d. It was worn by star player Pierre Turgeon, who came from the same hometown and was Crosby's idol growing up.

10. In what manner did the Penguins officially announce their color scheme change from their original look to the new black and gold combination in 1980?

    a. On television, during halftime of Super Bowl XIV

    b. On opening day, with a presentation on the team's jumbotron

    c. In the newspapers, with a press release sent to the Associated Press

    d. On a banner flown through the sky during the city's Fourth of July parade

11. The number 30 is traditionally worn by goalies. In Pittsburgh, 15 of the 16 players who have worn it played goaltender. Which one did not?

    a. Roberto Romano

    b. Paul Gardner

    c. Alain Chevrier

    d. Gord Laxton

12. Mario Lemieux is the only Penguin to have ever worn the number 66 on his jersey.

    a. True

    b. False

13. Why did superstar Jaromir Jagr choose to wear number 68 on the back of his jersey?

    a. To show that he had arrived after Mario Lemieux, but was close to the same talent level as the Great 66.

    b. He was born on June 8, 1968.

    c. In honor of a political uprising called the Prague Spring that happened in his home country, Czechoslovakia, in 1968.

    d. It was the inverse of 86, which was his favorite number but was not available as another player was already wearing it when he joined the team.

14. How many jersey numbers have the Pittsburgh Penguins retired for their former players?

    a. 0

    b. 1

    c. 2

    d. 5

15. Which Hall of Fame defenseman is the only player ever to wear number 77 for the Penguins?

    a. Paul Coffey

    b. Randy Carlyle

    c. Ron Stackhouse

    d. Larry Murphy

16. Prior to 1995, NHL teams were not generally allowed to design and wear their own third jerseys. However, the Penguins used a gold jersey, which they wore specifically for Sunday games for a few years in the early 1980s.

a. True

b. False

17. Lucky number 7 has been worn by 17 Penguins players over the years. Which skater wore it for the longest amount of time?

    a. Joe Mullen

    b. Rod Buskas

    c. Paul Martin

    d. Russ Anderson

18. What was the number "250" in reference to when the Penguins added a gold "Pittsburgh 250" patch on the shoulders of their jerseys for the 2007 season?

    a. For the 250 career goals scored by captain Sidney Crosby, which he reached in the final game of 2006

    b. For the 250,000 total fans who had attended the team's playoff home games the year before

    c. The 250th anniversary of the foundation of the city of Pittsburgh

    d. Recognition of the team's 2 Stanley Cup championship wins in its first 50 years

19. Which number did Ab McDonald, who was named the first captain in Penguins' history, wear on the back of his jersey?

    a. 1

    b. 3

    c. 9

    d. 20

20. After a small dressing room fire destroyed much of their equipment hours before game time on November 7, 1972, the Penguins were forced to skate in their match with 14 players in white jerseys and 6 players in blue jerseys.

    a. True
    b. False

QUIZ ANSWERS

1. C – Dark blue, light blue, and white

2. B – False

3. D – He passed away as a result of a car crash after finishing second in rookie of the year voting for the Penguins.

4. B – Boston Bruins

5. D – The word "Pittsburgh" written diagonally across the chest

6. C – 23

7. B – False

8. B – Aleksey Morozov

9. C – He was born on August 7, 1987.

10. A – On television, during halftime of Super Bowl XIV

11. B – Paul Gardner

12. A – True

13. C – In honor of a political uprising called the Prague Spring that happened in his home country in 1968.

14. C – 2

15. A – Paul Coffey

16. A – True

17. B – Rod Buskas

18. C – The 250th anniversary of the foundation of the city of Pittsburgh

19. D – 20

20. B – False

DID YOU KNOW?

1. The triangle displayed behind the skating penguin in Pittsburgh's logo represents the city's "Golden Triangle" business district, which is formed by the confluence of two of the city's major rivers (Allegheny and Monongahela) into a third river (Ohio).

2. The highest number ever sported by a Penguins goaltender is 92. Tomas Vokoun wore it during the 2013 season after arriving in a trade from the Washington Capitals. He decided to flip the digits in his usual number, 29, after realizing that incumbent Pens goalie Marc-Andre Fleury was already wearing 29.

3. The Penguins changed to a black and gold color scheme in part to synchronize with the city's other successful sports teams (the NFL's Steelers, and MLB's Pirates). However, they also made the change because the flag of Pittsburgh features black and gold stripes.

4. Some numbers have proven unpopular with Pittsburgh players. Twenty numbers have gone unused in franchise history, as no Penguin has ever worn a jersey with the following numbers: 0, 00, 64, 69, 70, 78, 79, 80, 83, 84, 86, 88, 89, 90, 91, 94, 96, 97, 98, or 99.

5. When Penguins right winger Pierre-Luc Letourneau-Leblond made it to the NHL, he became the player with the longest full name in NHL history. Luckily for the

equipment staff, he opted to wear just "Leblond" on the back of his number 32 jersey.

6. When the team revamped its logo for the 1992-93 season, they tried to modernize the Penguin on their crest by simplifying and streamlining it. The result received mixed reviews and was not exactly embraced by fans. It was widely referred to as the "Robo-Penguin" but lasted until the 2002-03 season when Pittsburgh brought back a version closer to the original Penguin.

7. Superstition may have scared some Penguins away from wearing the number 13. Only seven players in franchise history have chosen it for themselves, and only one, Jim Hamilton, wore it for more than two seasons.

8. Throwback blue jerseys worn by the Penguins during the 2008-2013 era were dubbed the "Blue Jerseys of Doom" by the Pittsburgh Tribune-Review because, although the Penguins wore them sparingly, they happened to have them on when Sidney Crosby suffered a broken jaw, again when he suffered a concussion, and again when Evgeni Malkin was concussed later.

9. Top defenseman Kris Letang wears number 58 for the Penguins. When he agreed to a contract extension with the team in 2013, he and his agent negotiated it to be for $58 million over eight years.

10. Five players have worn number 55 for the Penguins, and all of them were defensemen. Larry Murphy was the first, followed by Drake Berehowsky, Ric Jackman, Sergei Gonchar, and Philip Samuelsson.

CHAPTER 3:

CATCHY NICKNAMES

QUIZ TIME!

1. By which franchise nickname are the Penguins most commonly referred to?

   a. Frosties

   b. Pens

   c. Oreos

   d. Guins

2. Due to his last name, the similarity of Penguins and Herons, both being birds, and Pittsburgh's blue jerseys, goaltender Denis Herron was referred to as "The Blue Herron."

   a. True

   b. False

3. The longtime home of the Penguins, Mellon Arena (formerly Civic Arena and Civic Auditorium) was also more commonly known by which shape-inspired nickname?

   a. The Pittsburgh Zoo

   b. The Arctic Circle

c. The North Pole

d. The Igloo

4. Which three forwards played together in a combination known as "The Firing Line"?

   a. Mario Lemieux, Jaromir Jagr, and Ron Francis
   b. Martin Straka, Kevin Stevens, and Mark Recchi
   c. Evgeni Malkin, James Neal, and Chris Kunitz
   d. Dan Quinn, Joe Mullen, and Randy Cunneyworth

5. Early Penguins left winger John Robert Kelly was often referred to by which rugged nickname?

   a. Granite Block
   b. Battleship
   c. Commando
   d. Lumberjack

6. Which of the following is not a nickname that was given to Penguins winger James Neal?

   a. Lazy
   b. The Real Deal
   c. The Whitby Wizard
   d. Jimmy Hockey

7. Winger Joe Mullen was called "Slippery Rock Joe" for his agility in avoiding hits and balance when absorbing them (which he partially developed through playing roller hockey as a child).

   a. True
   b. False

8. Why was Jordan Staal given the nickname "Gronk" by teammate Colby Armstrong?

    a. He closely physically resembled New England Patriot star tight end Rob Gronkowski.

    b. His coaches had once remarked in practice that he was "great on his skates, and strong as a donkey."

    c. He made a grunting sound every time he threw a body check, which Armstrong believed sounded like "Gronk."

    d. He had a very strong presence, like a Marvel comic book villain of the same name.

9. Why was the forward trio of Syl Apps, Jean Pronovost, and Lowell McDonald known collectively as "The Century Line"?

    a. As veterans, their ages added together to equal more than 100 years.

    b. Each one's contract was signed for $100,000 per year.

    c. They totaled more than 100 goals for four consecutive seasons.

    d. Each one of them recorded more than 100 penalty minutes during their first season together.

10. For what reason did Penguins fans refer to goaltender Johan Hedberg as "Moose"?

    a. He was late for practice one day after being delayed by hitting a moose with his car on the highway.

    b. He had a moose painted on his goalie mask from his time with the minor league Manitoba Moose.

c. He challenged opposing players who crashed the net by headbutting them, as if he were a moose using its antlers.

d. He was the strongest member of the team in the weight room and could bench press heavier amounts than anyone else.

11. Which Penguins player was known to fans and teammates by the nickname "Whitey"?

    a. Mark Eaton
    b. Greg Polis
    c. Ken Schinkel
    d. Wayne Bianchin

12. Pittsburgh forward Brandon Sutter received the nickname "Flat Stanley" after a famous book series because he was very thin when he first arrived with the team.

    a. True
    b. False

13. Although he refuses to reveal its origins, Pens defenseman Douglas Murray goes by which interesting nickname?

    a. Bulldozer
    b. Crankshaft
    c. Tsunami Doug
    d. Smash & Grab

14. Why did teammates call Penguins forward Matt Cullen by the nickname "Dad"?

    a. He is the father of three sons.

b. He is known throughout the locker room for giving advice and safety tips.

c. He is 42 years old; old enough to be the father of some teammates.

d. He once yelled "Who's your Daddy?" at an opposing team after scoring a goal.

15. Franchise icon Sidney Crosby is so good that he has several nicknames, such as "The Next One" (in reference to being as good as Wayne "The Great One" Gretzky) and "Creature" (in reference to his muscular lower body). But what is his most widely known and used nickname?

a. Sid the Kid

b. The Crosby Show

c. Highlight Reel

d. East Coast Eddie

16. Penguins winger Kevin Stevens shared the same nickname as his father, Arthur "Artie" Stevens.

a. True

b. False

17. Why was the 1990-91 forward combination of John Cullen, Mark Recchi, and Kevin Stevens known as "The Option Line"?

a. They were equally effective whether they were at even strength, killing penalties, or on the power play.

b. They were the coach's favorite option to put on the ice when the Penguins needed to close out tight games.

c. They could all switch positions between center, left wing, and right wing.

d. They were all playing that season while in the final year of their contracts.

18. While with Pittsburgh, defenseman Larry Murphy became known for something called the "Murphy Dump." What was this?

a. A sneaky move used to trip an opponent with his knee without drawing a penalty

b. An intentional giveaway of the puck to a forechecking forward, whom he would immediately flatten with a body check

c. A high, arcing loft of the puck over opponents' heads which cleared the zone but stopped short of drawing an icing call

d. A shot into the opponents' zone designed to bank off the boards and settle behind the goalie's net for a Penguins winger to chase down

19. Penguins tough guy Paul Bissonnette went by which nickname, both on the ice and on his social media accounts?

a. BizNasty

b. The Beast

c. Fist Face

d. Banger

20. Penguins father and son duo Greg and Ryan Malone both wore the number 12 with the team, and both went by the

nickname "Bugsy" after a 1976 gangster film that was popular when Greg was a player.

a. True

b. False

QUIZ ANSWERS

1. B – Pens

2. B – False

3. D – The Igloo

4. C – Evgeni Malkin, James Neal, and Chris Kunitz

5. B – Battleship

6. D – Jimmy Hockey

7. A – True

8. D – He had a very strong presence, like a Marvel comic book villain of the same name.

9. C – They totaled more than 100 goals for four consecutive seasons.

10. B – He had a moose painted on his goalie mask from his time with the minor league Manitoba Moose.

11. C – Ken Schinkel

12. A – True

13. B – Crankshaft

14. C – He is 42 years old; old enough to be the father of some teammates.

15. A – Sid the Kid

16. A – True

17. D – They were all playing that season while in the final year of their contracts.

18. C – A high, arcing loft of the puck over opponents' heads which cleared the zone but stopped short of drawing an icing call

19. A – BizNasty

20. A – True

DID YOU KNOW?

1. The "Penguins" nickname was selected for the franchise as the result of a contest. Seven hundred entries nominated the name, primarily because their pre-existing arena was already known locally as "The Igloo."

2. Penguins defender Rob Scuderi was saddled with the nickname "The Piece" after accidentally telling reporters he was "the missing piece" (as opposed to "a piece") of the Penguins puzzle. His teammates did not let this go easily.

3. Penguin winger Beau Bennett was nicknamed "Sunshine" after a character in a Disney movie called *Remember the Titans*. Bennett slightly resembled the character, and also came from California as the character did.

4. Marc-Andre Fleury goes by the nickname "Flower," which is an English translation of his last name. His goalie masks have occasionally shown off some flower artwork and always display a fleur-de-lis.

5. When Jaromir Jagr came to Pittsburgh after the 1990 NHL Draft, it was astutely noticed that his first name could be made into the anagram "Mario Jr." This was quite fitting as he teamed with Mario Lemieux to lead the Penguins to great accomplishments.

6. Forward Nick Bjugstad was interestingly nicknamed "Rotisserie Chicken" after skipping dinner with some teammates and picking up his own rotisserie chicken at a

supermarket instead. Some amused fans threw chicken wings on the ice when they learned of the nickname.

7. One-time Penguins goaltender Wendell Young is known as "The Ringmaster." He earned the name when he became the only hockey player in history to win the Memorial Cup, the Turner Cup, the Calder Cup, and the Stanley Cup.

8. Mario Lemieux was known by two nicknames: "Super Mario" came from a popular Nintendo video game called Super Mario Bros. and was an easy combination of his talent and first name. "Le Magnifique" was bestowed upon him for its alliterative qualities and his French-Canadian heritage.

9. Forward Aleksey Morozov was known as "The Devil Killer" because of his prowess in games against the New Jersey Devils. Devils goalie Martin Brodeur remarked that he had nightmares of Morozov and stated, "The guy's in my kitchen. He's in my head. I can't get rid of him."

10. Pens winger Phil Bourque became a color commentator for the team where he is known by fans as "Ol' Two-Niner," which references his uniform number with the club. He hosts a pregame interview segment called "Two Minutes with the Ol' Two-Niner," in which he speaks with a person relevant to the upcoming contest before each broadcast.

CHAPTER 4:

THE CAPTAIN CLASS

QUIZ TIME!

1. Which veteran player was honored by being named the inaugural captain of the Pittsburgh Penguins in 1967?

   a. Jean Pronovost

   b. Syl Apps

   c. Ab McDonald

   d. Peter Lee

2. The Penguins went through five captains before finally naming someone who would remain with the team for more than a single season.

   a. True

   b. False

3. Earl Ingarfield, Pittsburgh's second captain, tallied 60 points in 90 games with the club before being traded to which other NHL club?

   a. New York Rangers

   b. St. Louis Blues

c. New York Islanders

d. Oakland Seals

4. Which player briefly remained captain of the Penguins even after franchise savior Mario Lemieux returned from retirement in 2001, before Lemieux eventually regained his captaincy?

a. Jaromir Jagr

b. Ron Francis

c. Mark Recchi

d. John LeClair

5. For how many consecutive seasons did captain Randy Carlyle lead all Penguins defensemen in scoring?

a. 1

b. 3

c. 5

d. 7

6. Mike Bullard, who captained the Penguins for three years, went on to play and coach in many European countries after his career in the NHL ended. Which country did he not work in?

a. Switzerland

b. Sweden

c. Germany

d. Austria

7. Ron Francis was the captain of the Penguins when he scored the Stanley Cup-clinching goal against the Chicago Blackhawks in Game 4 of the 1992 Finals.

a. True

b. False

8. Although he was born in Canada, Pittsburgh captain Orest Kindrachuk's first language was neither English nor French. Instead, he spoke which language as his primary choice?

a. German

b. Czechoslovakian

c. Russian

d. Ukrainian

9. Which Penguins captain served for only two months before tearing a ligament and handing the "C" over to a young Mario Lemieux?

a. Terry Ruskowski

b. Ron Francis

c. Dan Frawley

d. Mike Bullard

10. Which Penguins captain ranks second on the NHL's all-time points list, behind only the legendary Wayne Gretzky?

a. Sidney Crosby

b. Mario Lemieux

c. Ron Francis

d. Jaromir Jagr

11. How many times did prolific Penguins captain Jean Pronovost score 40 (or more) goals in a single season?

a. 0

b. 1

c. 2

d. 4

12. For three seasons in the 1980s, Pittsburgh elected not to name a captain. Instead, they had a rotation of players wear an "A" (usually designated for assistant captains) with three sporting the letter in each game.

   a. True

   b. False

13. Which captain did the Penguins trade to the Winnipeg Jets to complete a deal in which they received Doug Bodger and Moe Mantha in return?

   a. Ron Francis

   b. Orest Kindrachuk

   c. Randy Carlyle

   d. Mike Bullard

14. Penguins captain Jean Pronovost had two brothers, named Marcel and Claude, who also played in the NHL, amassing over 2,000 games played between them. How many of these NHL games did Claude Pronovost play?

   a. 3

   b. 30

   c. 300

   d. 1,300

15. Which Penguins captain played for the Houston Aeros of the WHA before his time in Pittsburgh, and is a member of the World Hockey Association Hall of Fame?

a. Jean Pronovost

b. Earl Ingarfield

c. Mario Lemieux

d. Terry Ruskowski

16. During their entire history, the Pittsburgh Penguins have only elected one defenseman to be the captain of the team.

a. True

b. False

17. One Penguins captain has played for nine NHL teams, more than any other franchise leader. Who was this well-traveled player?

a. Jaromir Jagr

b. Ron Francis

c. Earl Ingarfield

d. Randy Carlyle

18. Randy Carlyle is the only Penguins captain ever to win which of the following awards?

a. King Clancy Memorial Trophy

b. James Norris Memorial Trophy

c. Maurice "Rocket" Richard Trophy

d. Conn Smythe Trophy

19. Which Penguins captain finished in the second spot on the NHL's all-time assists list, trailing only Wayne Gretzky for most helpers ever?

a. Sidney Crosby

b. Mario Lemieux

c. Ron Francis

d. Jaromir Jagr

20. In Mario Lemieux and Sidney Crosby, the Penguins boast the two longest-serving captains (measured by seasons played while captain of the team) in NHL history.

a. True

b. False

QUIZ ANSWERS

1. C – Ab McDonald

2. B – False

3. D – Oakland Seals

4. A – Jaromir Jagr

5. C – 5

6. B – Sweden

7. B – False

8. D – Ukrainian

9. C – Dan Frawley

10. D – Jaromir Jagr

11. D – 4

12. B – False

13. C – Randy Carlyle

14. A – 3

15. D – Terry Ruskowski

16. A – True

17. A – Jaromir Jagr

18. B – James Norris Memorial Trophy

19. C – Ron Francis

20. B – False

DID YOU KNOW?

1. The Penguins named six captains who had played elsewhere before coming to Pittsburgh. The first one drafted and developed by the team was Mike Bullard, who was selected 9th overall in the 1980 NHL Draft and became the Penguins captain in 1984.

2. At a hockey banquet in St. Louis, Blues center Ron Schock was asked which NHL city would be his least favorite destination if he were traded. He replied that he would not like to go to the New York Rangers or Pittsburgh Penguins. Two days afterward, the Penguins traded for him and eventually named him their captain.

3. Dan Frawley remains the only Penguins captain ever born with an Indigenous background. He is a member of the Ojibwe people and comes from Nipissing First Nation. Frawley played with Pittsburgh for four seasons before returning to the minor leagues.

4. In 2014, former Penguins captain Ron Francis was named general manager of the Carolina Hurricanes. He replaced former Penguins player Jim Rutherford, who left the Hurricanes position and became general manager of Pittsburgh instead.

5. During the 1975-76 season, talented captain Jean Pronovost became the first Penguin to score 50 goals, and also the first Penguin to record 100 points in a single year.

6. Penguins center Terry Ruskowski was known for his leadership qualities. In addition to being captain of the Pens, he also served as captain for the Houston Aeros, Los Angeles Kings, and Winnipeg Jets. He is one of only two men in history, the other being Wayne Gretzky, to wear the captain "C" for four major professional hockey clubs.

7. During the twenty-year period between 1981 and 2001, only three players won the Art Ross Trophy as the NHL's leading scorer. Two of them were Penguins captains: Mario Lemieux and Jaromir Jagr. The other was Wayne Gretzky.

8. Orest Kindrachuk, who captained the Penguins from 1978-81, played for three NHL teams during his career. In addition to the Pens, he also played for Pittsburgh's two biggest rivals, the Philadelphia Flyers and Washington Capitals; although, Kindrachuk was not named captain for either Philadelphia or Washington.

9. Penguins captain Jaromir Jagr represented his nation in men's ice hockey during five separate Winter Olympics from 1998-2014, winning one gold and one bronze medal. Jagr was also honored by being asked to serve as the flag bearer for his country, the Czech Republic, at the 2010 Winter Olympics in Vancouver.

10. Mario Lemieux has served the longest combined tenure as Penguins captain. His reign was broken into three stints (1987-1994, 1995-1997, and 2001-2006) due to illness and retirement.

CHAPTER 5:

STATISTICALLY SPEAKING

QUIZ TIME!

1. What is Pittsburgh's franchise record for most victories recorded by the club in a single regular season?

   a. 50
   b. 51
   c. 53
   d. 56

2. Three times in his career, workhorse goalie Marc-Andre Fleury played 67 games during a season, setting, and then matching, the Penguins' record each time.

   a. True
   b. False

3. In 1992-93, Pittsburgh set the NHL record (which they still own) for most consecutive games won. How many victories in a row did they produce?

   a. 12
   b. 15

c. 17

d. 21

4. How many times in his career did Mario Lemieux score three goals, or more, in a game to record a hat trick?

   a. 10

   b. 20

   c. 30

   d. 40

5. Which Penguins rookie set the modern NHL record by scoring a goal in his first six consecutive games at the beginning of his career?

   a. Mario Lemieux

   b. Sidney Crosby

   c. Kevin Stevens

   d. Evgeni Malkin

6. Four hundred and nine penalty minutes are the most recorded in any season by a Penguins player. Who spent enough time in the penalty box to establish this club record?

   a. Paul Baxter

   b. Kevin Stevens

   c. Dave Schultz

   d. Rick Tocchet

7. Mario Lemieux is the only Penguin to ever score more than 200 points in a season. He accomplished the feat three times during his career.

   a. True

   b. False

8. Which goaltender holds the Pittsburgh record for most wins in a single season, with 43 victories posted?

   a. Marc-Andre Fleury
   b. Matt Murray
   c. Johan Hedberg
   d. Tom Barrasso

9. Which Penguin has played more NHL games with the franchise than any other player?

   a. Sidney Crosby
   b. Mario Lemieux
   c. Kris Letang
   d. Rick Kehoe

10. The magnificent Mario Lemieux is Pittsburgh's all-time leader in goals scored. How many times did he score a goal for the team?

    a. 538
    b. 592
    c. 617
    d. 690

11. When the Penguins beat the Minnesota North Stars in Game 6 to win the 1991 Stanley Cup, they won by the largest margin of victory in several decades. What was the final score of that deciding game?

    a. 6-1
    b. 9-2
    c. 8-0
    d. 12-3

12. If you added Jaromir Jagr and Paul Coffey's assists with the Penguins together, they would still not equal Mario Lemieux's total.

    a. True
    b. False

13. Which Penguins defenseman has recorded the most points while playing with the club?

    a. Paul Coffey
    b. Kris Letang
    c. Randy Carlyle
    d. Sergei Gonchar

14. Three players in Pittsburgh history have higher shooting percentage accuracy with the team than the great Mario Lemieux. Which of the following does not?

    a. Petr Nedved
    b. Rob Brown
    c. Mike Bullard
    d. Joe Mullen

15. How many Penguins have fired over 2,000 shots on net for the club during their careers?

    a. 2
    b. 4
    c. 7
    d. 10

16. Sidney Crosby scored two points in the final game of his rookie season, giving him 102 points on the season and

pushing him ahead of Mario Lemieux for the highest total ever reached by a Penguins rookie.

a. True

b. False

17. Which Penguin recorded the highest career plus/minus with the Penguins, with a +207?

a. Kris Letang

b. Jaromir Jagr

c. Larry Murphy

d. Evgeni Malkin

18. Which Penguin recorded the most game-winning goals for the team, scoring 78 clutch markers to claim victory for the squad?

a. Mario Lemieux

b. Evgeni Malkin

c. Jaromir Jagr

d. Sidney Crosby

19. Where does Penguins icon Mario Lemieux rank on the all-time list for most points per game in the NHL?

a. 1st

b. 2nd

c. 8th

d. 66th

20. Goalie Denis Herron's 1977-78 season is the benchmark in terms of shots faced, as he faced 2,125; the only time a

Penguins goaltender has seen more than 2,000 shots in a season.

a. True
b. False

QUIZ ANSWERS

1. D – 56

2. A – True

3. C – 17

4. D – 40

5. D – Evgeni Malkin

6. A – Paul Baxter

7. B – False

8. D – Tom Barrasso

9. A – Sidney Crosby

10. D – 690

11. C – 8-0

12. A – True

13. B – Kris Letang

14. D – Joe Mullen

15. C – 7

16. A – True

17. B – Jaromir Jagr

18. C – Jaromir Jagr

19. B – 2nd

20. A – True

DID YOU KNOW?

1. Four players have scored more than 1,000 points with the Penguins franchise. Mario Lemieux leads the way with 1,723, and he is joined in that elite group by Sidney Crosby, Jaromir Jagr, and Evgeni Malkin.

2. On New Year's Eve, 1988, Mario Lemieux scored a goal in every possible way (shorthanded, on the power play, at even strength, on a penalty shot, and into an empty net). He was the only NHL player to ever achieve this feat.

3. Not counting seasons shortened by a lockout, the 1997-98 Penguins were the stingiest version of the club to ever take the ice. They allowed only 188 goals against during the entire year.

4. In their inaugural season, the Penguins finished 27-34-13. That was good for fifth place in their division, but did not qualify them for the playoffs. After that season, the team lost its leading goal scorer, Ab McDonald, in a trade, and its leading point-getter, Andy Bathgate, to retirement.

5. Of Mario Lemieux's 690 career goals, he scored 405 while playing at even-strength, 236 while on the power play, and 49 while shorthanded. All of those marks are Penguins records.

6. In the 2006-07 season, the Penguins had been rebuilt around the spectacular duo of Sidney Crosby and Evgeni Malkin. The team recorded over 100 points for the first

time in more than a decade and improved on the previous year's total by a whopping 47 points.

7. Marc-Andre Fleury dominates the Penguins' record books for goaltenders. He leads the franchise in: games played, wins, losses, ties, goals against, goals against average, shots faced, minutes played, and saves made.

8. The last time the Penguins scored more than 300 goals in a season was 1995-96, when they tallied 362. This was not far off from the team record, 367, set in 1992-93.

9. Only one Penguin has recorded more than 1,000 career penalty minutes for Pittsburgh. Kevin Stevens was just shy of the mark after his initial stint with the club from 1987-95. But he returned to the team from 2000-2002 and finished with 1,048.

10. In 1995-96, Jaromir Jagr fired 403 shots on the net, establishing the Penguins' record for most shots taken by one player in a single season. He scored 62 times, which was unsurprisingly also a career high for him.

CHAPTER 6:

THE TRADE MARKET

QUIZ TIME!

1. The very first trade ever made by the Pittsburgh Penguins occurred on June 6, 1967, when the Penguins received four players from the New York Rangers. Which single player did they give up in return?

    a. Art Stratton
    b. Roy Edwards
    c. Larry Jeffrey
    d. Al McNeil

2. Just a few years after Pittsburgh joined the NHL as an expansion team, they made a trade with an even newer expansion team, giving the Vancouver Canucks an 8th round draft pick in exchange for the Canucks' agreement not to select certain Penguins in the expansion draft.

    a. True
    b. False

3. When the Penguins made a trade to solidify their goaltending situation, they acquired star netminder Tom

Barrasso, who helped them to two Stanley Cup victories. Which two players did they have to give up to get him?

    a. Doug Bodger and Darrin Shannon

    b. Bob Errey and John Cullen

    c. Ken Wregget and Darius Kasparaitis

    d. Bob Kelly and Keith McCreary

4. The Pittsburgh Penguins twice traded center Martin Straka, once after he did not produce many points and once in order to save the franchise some money. Which teams did they deal Straka to?

    a. New York Islanders and Florida Panthers

    b. Detroit Red Wings and Vancouver Canucks

    c. Tampa Bay Lightning and New York Rangers

    d. Ottawa Senators and Los Angeles Kings

5. Which two useful players did the Penguins acquire from the Atlanta Thrashers in 2008, helping to spur them on a run to the Stanley Cup Finals?

    a. Danny Heatley and Ty Conklin

    b. Marian Hossa and Pascal Dupuis

    c. Colby Armstrong and Erik Christensen

    d. Carl Hagelin and Patric Hornqvist

6. On February 27, 2007, the Penguins and Phoenix Coyotes exchanged two heavyweight pugilists in a trade. Which two feared enforcers were swapped between the clubs?

    a. Jared Boll and George Parros

    b. Riley Cote and David Clarkson

c. Dan Carcillo and Georges Laraque

d. Ian Laperriere and Colton Orr

7. The Los Angeles Kings once made a trade offer to Pittsburgh involving four players and $15 million dollars to try to acquire Mario Lemieux and pair him with Wayne Gretzky. The Penguins turned the offer down, stating that Lemieux would not be dealt at any price for fear of a fan revolt.

a. True

b. False

8. In 2012-13, the Penguins added several veterans to their roster to bolster their chances of going on a long playoff run. Which of the following was not a player they traded for at this time?

a. Jean-Luc Grand-Pierre

b. Jussi Jokinen

c. Brenden Morrow

d. Jarome Iginla

9. From which NHL team did Pittsburgh acquire star goalie Tom Barrasso in a trade, in 1988?

a. New Jersey Devils

b. Buffalo Sabres

c. Hartford Whalers

d. Detroit Red Wings

10. During the recent NHL Expansion Draft held when the Vegas Golden Knights entered the league, Pittsburgh sent

Vegas a 2nd round NHL Entry Draft pick for "expansion draft considerations." What were those considerations?

- a. Vegas promised not to select promising young forward Jake Guentzel.
- b. Vegas promised to select defenseman Nate Schmidt from the Washington Capitals, thus weakening Pittsburgh's divisional rival.
- c. Vegas promised not to select established but unprotected winger Chris Kunitz.
- d. Vegas promised to select Marc-Andre Fleury, to free up salary cap space for Pittsburgh and clear the crease for Matt Murray.

11. Which player was not part of the return that the Penguins received when they dealt superstar winger Jaromir Jagr to the Washington Capitals in 2001?

- a. Kris Beech
- b. Ross Lupaschuk
- c. Sergei Gonchar
- d. Michal Sivek

12. Pittsburgh has never, in its history, completed a trade with the New Jersey Devils.

- a. True
- b. False

13. When the Penguins acquired Alexei Kovalev from the Ottawa Senators for a 2011 conditional draft pick, what was the condition placed on the pick?

a. A 5th round pick if the Penguins miss the playoffs, 4th round pick if they lose in round 1, 3rd round pick if they lose in round 2, 2nd round pick if they lose in the conference finals, 1st round pick if they make the Stanley Cup Finals

b. A 2nd round pick if Kovalev scores 20 or more goals, otherwise a 3rd round pick

c. A 1st round pick if Kovalev re-signs with the Penguins after the season, otherwise a 2nd round pick

d. A 6th rounder if the Penguins advance past the 1st round of the playoffs and Kovalev plays a minimum of 50% of the 1st round games, otherwise a 7th rounder

14. The Penguins acquired which superstar defenseman from the Edmonton Oilers after the Oilers won the Stanley Cup in 1987?

    a. Paul Coffey
    b. Kevin Lowe
    c. Steve Smith
    d. Phil Housley

15. Who did the Penguins send to the Edmonton Oilers in exchange for goaltender Gilles Meloche after the 1984-85 season?

    a. Jeff Beukeboom
    b. Dave Semenko
    c. Marty McSorley
    d. Andy Moog

16. In August of 1993, the Penguins acquired enforcer Marty McSorley from the Los Angeles Kings. In February of 1994, the Penguins traded enforcer Marty McSorley...to the Los Angeles Kings.

    a. True
    b. False

17. Financial difficulties were a major factor that led to Pittsburgh trading talented winger Alexei Kovalev in 2003. They shed Kovalev's salary and received cash (and players) in return from which NHL team?

    a. Montreal Canadiens
    b. New York Rangers
    c. Florida Panthers
    d. Ottawa Senators

18. Before their Stanley Cup victory in the 2015-16 season, Pittsburgh traded defenseman Rob Scuderi to the Chicago Blackhawks for which player?

    a. Trevor Daley
    b. Carl Hagelin
    c. Conor Sheary
    d. Justin Schultz

19. In 2018, the Penguins completed their first-ever three-team trade, acquiring Vincent Dunn, Derick Brassard, Tobias Lindberg, and a 3rd round pick. The team sent out Ian Cole, Filip Gustavsson, Ryan Reaves, and draft picks in the 1st, 3rd, and 4th rounds. Who were the other two teams involved in the complicated deal?

a. New York Rangers and Detroit Red Wings

b. Anaheim Ducks and Dallas Stars

c. Los Angeles Kings and Tampa Bay Lightning

d. Ottawa Senators and Vegas Golden Knights

20. When the Penguins acquired star defenseman Paul Coffey from the Edmonton Oilers in 1987, they gave up four defensemen in return, which was the most players from any specific position group included in any trade in NHL history.

a. True

b. False

QUIZ ANSWERS

1. C – Larry Jeffrey

2. A – True

3. A – Doug Bodger and Darrin Shannon

4. D – Ottawa Senators and Los Angeles Kings

5. B – Marian Hossa and Pascal Dupuis

6. C – Dan Carcillo and Georges Laraque

7. B – False

8. A – Jean-Luc Grand-Pierre

9. B – Buffalo Sabres

10. D – Vegas promised to select Marc-Andre Fleury, to free up salary cap space for Pittsburgh and clear the crease for Matt Murray.

11. C – Sergei Gonchar

12. B – False

13. D – A 6th rounder if the Penguins advance past the 1st round of the playoffs and Kovalev plays a minimum of 50% of the 1st round games, otherwise a 7th rounder

14. A – Paul Coffey

15. C – Marty McSorley

16. A – True

17. B – New York Rangers

18. A – Trevor Daley

19. D – Ottawa Senators and Vegas Golden Knights

20. B – False

DID YOU KNOW?

1. In 1977, the Penguins completed a four-player trade with the Montreal Canadiens, which was very Peter-centric. The Habs sent Pittsburgh forwards Peter Lee and Peter Mahovlich, while the Penguins sent Montreal forwards Peter Marsh and Pierre (the French form of Peter) Larouche.

2. In 1978, Pittsburgh had some financial concerns. To help address those, the Penguins made seven separate transactions on June 15 with the St. Louis Blues. The Penguins traded the Blues draft picks in the 7th, 9th, 10th, 11th, 12th, 13th, and 14th rounds. No players or picks were sent back; Pittsburgh acquired cash in each deal.

3. The 1st overall draft pick that the Penguins used to draft franchise superstar Sidney Crosby in 2005 was obtained through a previous trade with the Florida Panthers.

4. Pittsburgh and Buffalo have a rich history of trades throughout the years. Significant names moved between the two teams include: Rene Robert, Eddie Shack, Ted Nolan, Randy Cunneyworth, Doug Bodger, Tom Barrasso, Bob Errey, Mike Ramsey, Stu Barnes, and Matthew Barnaby.

5. An important trade between the Penguins and rival Flyers had major implications for the early 1990s Penguins playoff success. Pittsburgh sent star winger Mark Recchi to Philadelphia, but received help at three positions, bringing

back goalie Ken Wregget, defenseman Kjell Samuelsson, and forward Rick Tocchet.

6. Though the Penguins and Philadelphia Flyers are natural geographic rivals who play in the same division, they have not been scared to make big deals with each other. The two teams have made swaps involving at least seven assets (draft picks and players) three times; in 1976, 1983, and 1992.

7. One of the worst trades made by the Penguins occurred in 1996 when they sent a young Markus Naslund to the Vancouver Canucks in exchange for Alek Stojanov. Naslund went on to captain the Canucks for 8 years and played in 5 All-Star Games, while Stojanov played only 45 games with the Penguins before finishing his career in the minor leagues.

8. Defender Ian Moran learned that he had been traded from Pittsburgh to Boston in 2003. At the time he heard the news, he was outside playing hopscotch with his daughter in their driveway and had to jot down the Bruins' general manager's phone number on the ground in chalk.

9. The most recent trade made by Pittsburgh was to re-acquire forward Conor Sheary from the Buffalo Sabres. The Penguins sent Dominik Kahun to Buffalo for Sheary and Evan Rodrigues, after trading Sheary and Matt Hunwick there for a 4th round pick as part of a cost-cutting move in 2018.

10. The largest trade (by number of assets) ever completed by

the Penguins was consummated in 2015 with the Toronto Maple Leafs. Pittsburgh acquired Phil Kessel, Tim Erixon, Tyler Biggs, and a 2nd round draft pick while giving up Kasperi Kapanen, Scott Harrington, Nick Spaling, a 1st round draft pick, and a 3rd round draft pick.

CHAPTER 7:

DRAFT DAY

QUIZ TIME!

1. When the city of Pittsburgh hosted the NHL Entry Draft in 2012, which prospect did the Penguins draft with their 1st round pick in front of the hometown fans?

    a. Olli Maatta

    b. Matt Murray

    c. Tyler Kennedy

    d. Jake Guentzel

2. The Penguins may have seen a positional need in their most recent NHL Draft. In 2019, the team used their five picks to select four right wingers and one defenseman.

    a. True

    b. False

3. How high did Pittsburgh select defenseman Ryan Whitney in the 2002 NHL Entry Draft?

    a. 1st round, 5th overall

    b. 2nd round, 43rd overall

c. 4th round, 151st overall

d. 7th round, 222nd overall

4. Which goaltender did the Penguins select highest in the NHL Entry Draft, using a 1st overall pick to add the netminder to their team?

   a. Tom Barrasso

   b. Marc-Andre Fleury

   c. Vince Hermany

   d. Ken Wregget

5. The Penguins selected goaltender Al Smith in the NHL Intraleague Draft in 1969. Which organization did they claim him from?

   a. Toronto Maple Leafs

   b. Detroit Red Wings

   c. New York Rangers

   d. Chicago Blackhawks

6. Which forward did the Penguins opt to select with the 2nd overall pick in the 2006 NHL Draft?

   a. Nicklas Backstrom

   b. Phil Kessel

   c. Jordan Staal

   d. Jonathan Toews

7. Despite being drafted one year before Sidney Crosby, Evgeni Malkin did not make his Penguins debut before "Sid the Kid" because of a contract dispute with his team in Russia that left him ineligible to play for Pittsburgh immediately.

a. True

b. False

8. The Penguins have mined the OHL for talent frequently in the NHL Entry Draft, and have selected thirteen players from one specific OHL team, more than they have chosen from any other squad. Which team was it?

   a. Peterborough Petes

   b. Sault Ste. Marie Greyhounds

   c. London Knights

   d. Oshawa Generals

9. Which undrafted player did not learn to skate until he was ten years old, but still won two Stanley Cups with the Penguins and was elected to Hockey Hall of Fame?

   a. Dan Quinn

   b. Kevin Stevens

   c. Joe Mullen

   d. Ken Wregget

10. Who was the first player ever drafted by the Penguins that did not play for a Canadian junior team?

   a. Guido Tenesi

   b. Joe Noris

   c. Larry Bignell

   d. Paul Hoganson

11. The Anaheim Mighty Ducks selected which Pittsburgh Penguin in the 1993 Expansion Draft and then immediately named him as their first captain?

a. Max Talbot

b. Ryan Malone

c. Jiri Slegr

d. Troy Loney

12. The Penguins have selected just one player from the Canadian National team. They chose defenseman Zarley Zalapski in 1986.

a. True

b. False

13. NHL legend Jaromir Jagr was the first Czechoslovakian taken in the NHL Draft without defecting from his country first. Which pick did the Penguins take him with, in 1990?

a. 1st overall

b. 5th overall

c. 47th overall

d. 212th overall

14. Pittsburgh has selected 2nd overall in the NHL Entry Draft three times since the 1980s. Which of the following players was not selected with one of the 1st overall picks right in front of the Penguins' choice?

a. Wendel Clark

b. Erik Johnson

c. Jonathan Toews

d. Alexander Ovechkin

15. Superstar center Evgeni Malkin was drafted by Pittsburgh 2nd overall in the 2004 NHL Entry Draft. Which player was selected ahead of him?

a. Taylor Hall to the Edmonton Oilers

b. Erik Johnson to the St. Louis Blues

c. Sidney Crosby to the Pittsburgh Penguins

d. Alexander Ovechkin to the Washington Capitals

16. In 1984, the Detroit Red Wings had told defenseman Doug Bodger that they planned to draft him, and even asked him to wear a red tie. But on draft day, they passed, and the Penguins selected Bodger 9th overall.

a. True

b. False

17. Three times the Penguins have had the 1st overall pick in the NHL Draft, and every time they have selected a player from the QMJHL. Which of the following players was not selected with one of those picks?

a. Mario Lemieux

b. Jean Pronovost

c. Marc-Andre Fleury

d. Sidney Crosby

18. Which player did the Penguins lose to the Vegas Golden Knights in the 2017 NHL Expansion Draft?

a. Brian Dumoulin

b. Deryk Engelland

c. Marc-Andre Fleury

d. Matt Murray

19. What is the lowest position in the draft that the Penguins have selected a player who would go on to make the Hockey Hall of Fame?

a. 5th overall

b. 18th overall

c. 34th overall

d. 67th overall

20. Despite being selected 1st overall in the 1984 Draft and enjoying a Hall of Fame career, Mario Lemieux actually played fewer NHL games than defenseman Doug Bodger, who was drafted eight spots behind Lemieux by the Penguins in the same draft.

a. True

b. False

QUIZ ANSWERS

1. A – Olli Maatta

2. A – True

3. A – 1st round, 5th overall

4. B – Marc-Andre Fleury

5. A – Toronto Maple Leafs

6. C – Jordan Staal

7. A – True

8. D – Oshawa Generals

9. C – Joe Mullen

10. A – Guido Tenesi

11. D – Troy Loney

12. A – True

13. B – 5th overall

14. C – Jonathan Toews

15. D – Alexander Ovechkin to the Washington Capitals

16. A – True

17. B – Jean Pronovost

18. C – Marc-Andre Fleury

19. D – 67th overall, the player was Ulf Samuelsson

20. A – True

DID YOU KNOW?

1   Only three times in NHL history has a goaltender been selected 1st overall in the NHL Draft. Pittsburgh's Marc-Andre Fleury was the most recent goalie to reach that pinnacle when he was taken ahead of forwards Eric Staal and Nathan Horton in 2003.

2. Prior to the 1984 NHL Draft, which had Mario Lemieux available for the team that had the 1st overall pick, the Penguins shipped out veteran players and posted multiple six-game stretches without a single win. It was speculated by the rival New Jersey Devils that the Penguins were losing on purpose to secure Lemieux, but coach Lou Angotti did not admit this to be true until much later.

3. When the Penguins were formed and participated in the NHL's Expansion Draft, they made a wise selection in taking Ken Schinkel from the New York Rangers organization. Schinkel was immediately one of Pittsburgh's top scorers and made two NHL All-Star teams.

4. The Penguins have drafted two players from the city of Pittsburgh: defenseman James Mathers, with the 223rd overall pick in 1974, and Ryan Malone, with the 115th overall pick in 1999. Unfortunately, Mathers did not make it to the NHL, but Malone did, and played over 600 career NHL games.

5. Jaromir Jagr lasted until the 5th overall pick in the 1990

NHL Draft, where the Penguins selected him. Although the four players selected ahead of him had long and successful careers, Jagr eclipsed them all. He played at least a decade longer than Petr Nedved, Keith Primeau, and Mike Ricci, and eight seasons longer than 1st overall selection Owen Nolan.

6. In 2005, the Penguins won a lottery for the right to select Sidney Crosby 1st overall. Due to a lockout the previous year, every single NHL team was included in the lottery. The selection helped save hockey in Pittsburgh as interest and revenues both increased heavily after the pick.

7. The largest Penguins draft class ever was selected in 1975, when the team drafted 15 players over the course of the draft's eighteen rounds. Nine of those players never saw NHL action. Two of them played a handful of games without much success. Four of them lasted more than one season, with defenders Russ Anderson and Paul Baxter enjoying the most career success.

8. When the Penguins drafted Mario Lemieux amid much fanfare in 1984, he was locked in a contract dispute with the team. As a result, he refused to participate in the customary traditions of shaking hands with Pittsburgh general manager Eddie Johnston or putting on the team's jersey.

9. The Penguins did not draft well at the beginning of their NHL existence. In 1967, the team selected only two players, and neither ever played in the league. And 1968

was not much better, as Pittsburgh took three players. Two of them did skate in the NHL, but they only lasted for a combined 16 games.

10. The latest pick the Penguins have made in the NHL Draft was Swedish defenseman Hans Jonsson, 286th overall in 1993. Amazingly, Jonsson did play in the NHL for 242 games and had more success than some of the team's top 5 overall picks, like Steve Rexe and Gary Swain.

CHAPTER 8:

GOALTENDER TIDBITS

QUIZ TIME!

1. Who was the regular starting goalie for Pittsburgh during the team's difficult first season in the NHL?

    a. Denis Herron
    b. Les Binkley
    c. Gilles Meloche
    d. Jim Rutherford

2. Gilles Meloche played goaltender for the Penguins, and his son Eric later played for Pittsburgh as well, though as a right winger rather than a goalie.

    a. True
    b. False

3. Which goaltender has recorded the most career shutouts while with the Pittsburgh Penguins?

    a. Ken Wregget
    b. Matt Murray
    c. Marc-Andre Fleury
    d. Tom Barrasso

4. Wendell Young played goaltender for the Penguins in 1992 and 1994. In between, he played for three other professional teams. Which of the following did he not suit up for?

    a. Tampa Bay Lightning
    b. Atlanta Knights
    c. Chicago Wolves
    d. Wilkes-Barre / Scranton Penguins

5. Which Penguins goaltender faced (and saved) the first-ever playoff overtime penalty shot awarded in NHL history, keeping the Penguins alive for an eventual win?

    a. Tom Barrasso
    b. Matt Murray
    c. Gary Inness
    d. Ken Wregget

6. Which goaltender played for both the Pittsburgh Penguins and their main rivals, the Philadelphia Flyers and Washington Capitals?

    a. Casey DeSmith
    b. Denis Herron
    c. Gary Inness
    d. Jim Rutherford

7. It is a Penguins tradition for every goaltender to tap both posts and the crossbar with his stick following the warm-up before a game.

    a. True
    b. False

8. Former Penguins goaltender Al Smith wrote a play in his retirement about an ex-goalie who attends an art exhibit. The play was staged at Alumnae Theatre in Toronto. What was the play called?

   a. *Confessions to Anne Sexton*
   b. *The Art of Net-Minding*
   c. *Beauty Between the Pipes*
   d. *Murder at the Gala*

9. Which Penguins netminder holds the NHL record for most career points by a goalie, with 48?

   a. Marc-Andre Fleury
   b. Ken Wregget
   c. Tom Barrasso
   d. Denis Herron

10. Jean-Sebastien Aubin recorded his first NHL shutout against which NHL team?

    a. Tampa Bay Lightning
    b. Ottawa Senators
    c. Toronto Maple Leafs
    d. Boston Bruins

11. Goalie Denis Herron started and ended his NHL career with the Penguins. Which other teams did he play for in between his three separate stints with Pittsburgh?

    a. New York Rangers and New Jersey Devils
    b. Kansas City Scouts and Montreal Canadiens
    c. St. Louis Blues and Detroit Red Wings
    d. Vancouver Canucks and Boston Bruins

12. Tristan Jarry's goalie mask features a drawing of the *Penguins of Madagascar* playing hockey against *Tom and Jerry*.

    a. True
    b. False

13. Which Penguins goalie won the team's Michel Briere Rookie of the Year Award in 2016 and its Aldege Bastien Memorial Good Guy Award in 2018?

    a. Matt Murray
    b. Tristan Jarry
    c. Casey DeSmith
    d. Brent Johnson

14. How many consecutive playoff victories did Tom Barrasso record in 1992-93 to set the NHL record?

    a. 8
    b. 10
    c. 12
    d. 14

15. Which former Penguins goaltender became a successful sports commentator, working on broadcasts for the Ottawa Senators, Toronto Maple Leafs, and on CBC's *Hockey Night in Canada*?

    a. Jim Rutherford
    b. Les Binkley
    c. Greg Millen
    d. Johan Hedberg

16. Former Penguins goalie Michel Plasse was the first goaltender in professional hockey to score a goal.

    a. True
    b. False

17. Which Penguins teammate did goalie Marc-Andre Fleury live with as a young player?

    a. Stu Barnes
    b. Chris Kunitz
    c. Mario Lemieux
    d. Mark Recchi

18. Pittsburgh goaltender Johan Hedberg played in the 2002 Winter Olympics for which team?

    a. Germany
    b. Austria
    c. Switzerland
    d. Sweden

19. Which job did goaltender Les Binkley take with the Pittsburgh Penguins after retiring from his playing career?

    a. Management
    b. Scout
    c. Broadcaster
    d. Assistant Coach

20. Goalie Dunc Wilson was named team MVP in 1976-77, but lost his starting job the following year and was demoted to the minors two years later.

    a. True
    b. False

QUIZ ANSWERS

1. B – Les Binkley

2. A – True

3. C – Marc-Andre Fleury

4. D – Wilkes-Barre / Scranton Penguins

5. D – Ken Wregget

6. C – Gary Inness

7. B – False

8. A – *Confessions to Anne Sexton*

9. C – Tom Barrasso

10. D – Boston Bruins

11. B – Kansas City Scouts and Montreal Canadiens

12. A – True

13. A – Matt Murray

14. D – 14

15. C – Greg Millen

16. A – True

17. C – Mario Lemieux

18. D – Sweden

19. B – Scout

20. A – True

DID YOU KNOW?

1. Italian citizen and national team netminder Roberto Romano was between the pipes for Pittsburgh in 1983-84, and performed fairly well. The team took criticism for sending him down to the AHL in favor of a lesser performing goalie, but it later came to light that the team was trying to achieve the league's worst record in order to draft Mario Lemieux.

2. Penguins goalie Tom Barrasso was a standout from an early age. He was the only goalie to make the NHL directly out of high school, and still remains the league's youngest ever winner of the Vezina Trophy as the NHL's best goalie. He is also the youngest netminder to ever win the Calder Memorial Trophy as Rookie of the Year.

3. Pittsburgh goaltender Matt Murray emerged as a starter late in the 2016 NHL season. As a result, he retained his rookie eligibility for the 2017 NHL season. This quirk means that Murray is the only rookie goalie in league history with two Stanley Cup championships, and he also holds the rookie record for postseason wins, with 22.

4. During the 1991 NHL playoffs, backup goaltender Frank Pietrangelo made what came to be known as "The Save" against Peter Stastny of the New Jersey Devils to keep the Penguins alive. He followed this up with a shutout in Game 7, the team advanced, and Pittsburgh went on to win the Stanley Cup over the Minnesota North Stars.

5. As a rookie with the Penguins in 2003-04, Marc-Andre Fleury played well early in the season but was sent down to the QMJHL later in the year amidst speculation that he might trigger a $3 million contract bonus with his performance if he kept playing for Pittsburgh. Fleury offered to give up his bonus just to stay in the NHL, but this request was rejected.

6. Before becoming an NHL goaltender, former Penguin Michel Dion considered a career in Major League Baseball and actually played for the Montreal Expos' minor league affiliates for two seasons.

7. Current Penguins goalie Matt Murray holds the AHL record with 304 minutes and 11 seconds of consecutive shutout hockey. The streak gave him four straight shutouts, and he was just over a minute away from a fifth.

8. Goaltender Peter Skudra beat the odds to make it to the NHL and win 26 games with the Penguins. Skudra hails from Latvia, which has produced only about 40 NHL players in league history. Skudra is one of only five Latvian goaltenders to have played in the NHL.

9. Inaugural goaltender Les Binkley did not start his career in the NHL until the age of 31. He was the first player ever signed by the Penguins franchise and immediately became the first NHL goaltender to wear contact lenses in the league.

10. Rookie goaltender Tristan Jarry played the first two games of the 2016 NHL playoffs for Pittsburgh before being

returned to the minors when Matt Murray became healthy. Jarry received a Stanley Cup ring when the Penguins won that year, but did not play enough to qualify to have his name etched on the cup. In 2017, he received *another* Stanley Cup ring when the Penguins repeated, but once again did not play enough to get his name on the cup.

CHAPTER 9:

PENGUINS DEFENDERS

QUIZ TIME!

1. While playing for the Pittsburgh Penguins in the late 1970s, defenseman Russ Anderson married which famous woman?

    a. Actress Loni Anderson

    b. Folk-rock singer Cher

    c. Actress Elizabeth Montgomery

    d. Miss America winner Dorothy Benham

2. Before the Sedin twins starred in Vancouver, Pittsburgh's Ulf and Kjell Samuelsson became the first Swedish twin brothers to play together in the NHL.

    a. True

    b. False

3. Which star defenseman once missed six weeks of action with the team after he suffered a stroke?

    a. Paul Coffey

    b. Kris Letang

c. Randy Carlyle

d. Sergei Gonchar

4. Which former Penguin defenseman earned his pilot's license, ran his own flight school, and then became a captain with Hawaiian Airlines?

a. Rod Buskas

b. Paul Martin

c. Kevin Hatcher

d. Moe Mantha

5. Which former Penguin defender is the only player to win a Stanley Cup with both Sidney Crosby and Alexander Ovechkin?

a. Sergei Gonchar

b. Justin Schultz

c. Mike Green

d. Brooks Orpik

6. During the 2014-15 NHL season, defenseman Olli Maatta missed games with multiple ailments. Which of the following did not plague Maatta during the ill-fated year?

a. A neck tumor

b. A shoulder injury

c. A staph infection

d. Mumps

7. Ian Moran has played more minutes on the Penguins' blueline than any other defenseman.

a. True

b. False

8. A Penguin became the first Russian defenseman to score 200 NHL goals. Who was he?

   a. Darius Kasparaitis
   b. Michal Rozsival
   c. Sergei Gonchar
   d. Josef Melichar

9. Which Penguins defenseman tied an NHL record (shared with Bobby Orr, among others) by recording six assists in a single game?

   a. Ron Stackhouse
   b. Randy Carlyle
   c. Kris Letang
   d. Larry Murphy

10. After retiring, which Penguins defenseman remained in Pittsburgh and opened a sporting goods store named after himself?

    a. Chris Tamer
    b. Kjell Samuelsson
    c. Ian Cole
    d. Duane Rupp

11. Which Penguins stalwart idolized defenseman Tim Horton as a child and got the chance to play with his idol when Horton joined Pittsburgh in 1971-72?

    a. Randy Carlyle
    b. Dave Burrows
    c. Rod Buskas
    d. Bryan Watson

12. Penguins defenseman Olli Maatta claims that his favorite book is the English dictionary.

    a. True
    b. False

13. Defenseman Larry Murphy won back-to-back Stanley Cups twice; once with Pittsburgh, and once with which other NHL team?

    a. Los Angeles Kings
    b. Washington Capitals
    c. New Jersey Devils
    d. Detroit Red Wings

14. Pens defender Ulf Samuelsson skated on the edge between clean and dirty with his on-ice play and was not popular with opponents. Which of the following phrases was not used to describe him?

    a. "The most hated man in hockey."
    b. "The lowest form of human being."
    c. "A menace to the reputation of the NHL."
    d. "Someone whose play is all about 'trying to hurt you.'"

15. Rob Scuderi was such a reliable defensive player for the Penguins that he maintained his spot in the lineup despite a very lengthy scoreless stretch. How long did he go without a goal?

    a. 39 games
    b. 64 games

c. 88 games

d. 120 games

16. Pens defender Randy Hillier won a Stanley Cup with the team as both a player and an assistant coach.

   a. True

   b. False

17. In a 2013 incident, against the Boston Bruins, Penguins defender Brooks Orpik was punched in the head and concussed while lying on the ice. This resulted in a 15-game suspension for which Bruins player?

   a. Brad Marchand

   b. Shawn Thornton

   c. Zdeno Chara

   d. Milan Lucic

18. Which Penguin defenseman ranks 2nd all-time in goals, assists, and points by an NHL blueliner?

   a. Kris Letang

   b. Sergei Gonchar

   c. Zarley Zalapski

   d. Paul Coffey

19. A Penguins defender holds the record for most playoff hits in a career, falling just shy of 500 with 499. Which defender was this?

   a. Brooks Orpik

   b. Hal Gill

   c. Rob Scuderi

   d. Ron Stackhouse

20. Pens defender Sergei Gonchar won a Stanley Cup with the team as both a player and a development coach.

    a. True
    b. False

QUIZ ANSWERS

1. D – Miss America winner Dorothy Benham

2. B – False

3. B – Kris Letang

4. A – Rod Buskas

5. D – Brooks Orpik

6. C – A staph infection

7. B – False

8. C – Sergei Gonchar

9. A – Ron Stackhouse

10. D – Duane Rupp

11. B – Dave Burrows

12. A – True

13. D – Detroit Red Wings

14. C – "A menace to the reputation of the NHL."

15. D – 120 games

16. B – False

17. B – Shawn Thornton

18. D – Paul Coffey

19. A – Brooks Orpik

20. A – True

DID YOU KNOW?

1. Pittsburgh's Rob Scuderi got his name engraved on the Stanley Cup when the Penguins won in 2009 and became the first player from Long Island, New York, ever to do so.

2. Sergei Gonchar followed a popular hockey tradition when he accepted rookie Evgeni Malkin into his home in 2006. The two had been teammates in Russia, and the Penguins liked having newcomers live with veterans to learn strong work habits and adapt to their new environment. Fellow young star Sidney Crosby had lived with Mario Lemieux when he had first arrived in Pittsburgh.

3. Stalwart defensemen Dave Burrows and Randy Carlyle were once traded for one another. Burrows was sent to the Toronto Maple Leafs for Carlyle and then returned to play for Pittsburgh again a few years later.

4. Defenseman Rod Buskas left Pittsburgh as their all-time leader in penalty minutes (a record he no longer holds). He ended his NHL career as a Chicago Blackhawk, where he lost in the 1991-92 Stanley Cup Finals...to Pittsburgh.

5. Pens defender Doug Bodger has more career assists than any other defenseman born in British Columbia. He is second in goals and points (to Shea Weber), and third in games played (to Dan Hamhuis and Brent Seabrook).

6. In 2016, Penguins defender Kris Letang scored the Stanley Cup-winning goal against the San Jose Sharks. He also

became only the fourth player ever to get a point on every game-winning goal for each of his team's victories in the Finals.

7. Pens defenseman Kevin Hatcher is the older brother of another NHL defenseman, Derian. Both Hatcher brothers had distinguished NHL careers of over a decade, and both were inducted into the United States Hockey Hall of Fame in 2010.

8. Hard-hitting Penguins defenseman Darius Kasparaitis played in a Russian record 28 Olympic hockey games. He was given the title Honoured Master of Sports of the USSR and is a member of the Russian and Soviet Hockey Hall of Fame.

9. Pittsburgh defenseman Brooks Orpik was named after Penguins coach Herb Brooks. Orpik was born just a few months after Brooks led the United States to the "Miracle on Ice" victory over the Soviet Union in the Lake Placid Winter Olympics.

10. New Amsterdam Vodka created a drink named after Pens defenseman Ryan Whitney. "Pink Whitney" is a vodka with a pink-lemonade taste, and is a bestseller in the United States and Canada.

CHAPTER 10:

CENTERS OF ATTENTION

QUIZ TIME!

1. Which fellow Czech centered a line with Jaromir Jagr in both Pittsburgh and Washington?

   a. Jan Hrdina

   b. Ron Schock

   c. Michal Rozsival

   d. Robert Lang

2. Superstar Sidney Crosby is the first and only player in any of the four major North American sports to capture a scoring title before turning 20 years old.

   a. True

   b. False

3. Which Penguins center got his first NHL goal during his first NHL game, while taking his first NHL shift, on his first NHL shot?

   a. Sidney Crosby

   b. Ron Francis

c. Mario Lemieux

d. Evgeni Malkin

4. One Penguins center had many family members who also played in the NHL, including a father named Bryan, a brother named Dennis, and a son named Ron. Who was he?

    a. Pat Boutette

    b. Bryan Hextall Jr.

    c. Pierre Larouche

    d. Mike Bullard·

5. In 2010-11, Pens center Sidney Crosby led the team in points with 66, despite missing many games with injury. In the process, he established the NHL record for fewest games played while leading a team in scoring. How many games did he play?

    a. 70 games

    b. 64 games

    c. 55 games

    d. 41 games

6. What prevented Tyler Kennedy from joining his Penguins teammate Kris Letang in the NHL's YoungStars game in 2008?

    a. Lasik eye surgery

    b. Mononucleosis

    c. His wedding

    d. His grandfather's death

7. For part of his career, superstar center Mario Lemieux smoked approximately half a pack of cigarettes each day.

   a. True
   b. False

8. Which former Penguin center became the coach of the Finnish national hockey team?

   a. Doug Shedden
   b. George Ferguson
   c. Gregg Sheppard
   d. Dave Hannan

9. On April 25, 1989, Mario Lemieux scored four goals in one period, to give him five total goals in the game. This tied the record for most playoff goals scored in a single game. Which of these players is not tied with him?

   a. Reggie Leach
   b. Maurice Richard
   c. Darryl Sittler
   d. Jari Kurri

10. One hockey legend gave high praise to a Penguins center. "I met him, and I've seen him play. Unless you put two guys on him, he'll kill you in a game." Which legend said this about which Penguin?

    a. Maurice Richard, speaking about Mario Lemieux
    b. Gordie Howe, speaking about Sidney Crosby
    c. Wayne Gretzky, speaking about Evgeni Malkin
    d. Bobby Orr, speaking about Ron Francis

11. Which former Penguins center was named the general manager of the expansion Seattle franchise set to join the NHL in 2021?

    a. Robert Lang

    b. Gregg Sheppard

    c. Ron Francis

    d. Matt Cullen

12. On the play where Sidney Crosby scored his 100th NHL goal, Evgeni Malkin earned an assist, which was his 200th NHL point. Crosby asked Pittsburgh's trainer to cut the puck in half so each player could have a souvenir.

    a. True

    b. False

13. Pens center Jordan Staal had an excellent rookie season, during which he became the youngest player ever to accomplish which two things?

    a. Take part in an NHL fight, and record five points in one game

    b. Be selected to the All-Star team, and win the Calder Memorial Trophy

    c. Lead his team in ice time, and play all 82 games in a season

    d. Score on a penalty shot, and score a hat trick

14. Center Ron Francis had an exemplary 2014-15 season that saw him become the first NHL player to win which two trophies in the same season?

a. Art Ross Trophy and Conn Smythe Trophy

b. Frank J. Selke Trophy and Lady Byng Trophy

c. Maurice "Rocket" Richard Trophy and Bill Masterton Trophy

d. Hart Memorial Trophy and Lester B. Pearson Trophy

15. What prompted star Mario Lemieux's second (and final) retirement in 2006?

a. Desire to spend time with his family

b. A concussion suffered in a collision with an opponent

c. Development of an irregular heartbeat

d. Lack of success by the Penguins in the playoffs

16. Evgeni Malkin was the first Russian player in NHL history to be awarded the Conn Smythe Trophy.

a. True

b. False

17. Which Penguins center scored the game-winning goal against the Buffalo Sabres in front of a record crowd at the NHL's first Winter Classic?

a. Evgeni Malkin

b. Matt Cooke

c. Sidney Crosby

d. Jordan Staal

18. Pierre Larouche netted 53 goals with the Penguins in 1975-76. He also scored over 45 goals with two other teams, making him the only player in NHL history to accomplish the feat with three squads. Who were the other teams he achieved this with?

a. Hartford Whalers and St. Louis Blues

b. Montreal Canadiens and New York Rangers

c. Chicago Blackhawks and California Golden Seals

d. Boston Bruins and New York Rangers

19. Which Penguin center became the first player since the NHL's inaugural 1917-18 season to score a goal in six straight games at the beginning of his career?

a. Syl Apps

b. Brandon Sutter

c. Jordan Staal

d. Evgeni Malkin

20. Stanley Cup champion Maxime Talbot married Cynthia Phaneuf, a Canadian figure skating champion.

a. True

b. False

QUIZ ANSWERS

1. D – Robert Lang

2. A – True

3. C – Mario Lemieux

4. B – Bryan Hextall Jr.

5. D – 41 games

6. B – Mononucleosis

7. A – True

8. A – Doug Shedden

9. D – Jari Kurri

10. B – Gordie Howe, speaking about Sidney Crosby

11. C – Ron Francis

12. A – True

13. D – Score on a penalty shot, and score a hat trick

14. B – Frank J. Selke Trophy and Lady Byng Trophy

15. C – Development of an irregular heartbeat

16. A – True

17. C – Sidney Crosby

18. B – Montreal Canadiens and New York Rangers

19. D – Evgeni Malkin

20. A – True

DID YOU KNOW?

1. Pittsburgh's Syl Apps Jr. had a lot to live up to. His father was: an Olympic pole vaulter, Hall of Fame hockey player with the Toronto Maple Leafs, World War II veteran, and member of the Legislative Assembly of Ontario. Apps Jr. did well for himself, though, and was inducted into the Penguins Hall of Fame in 1994.

2. Penguins center Evgeni Malkin owned a restaurant called VIP Zone in his home country, Russia. Malkin designed the restaurant to be prison themed, so it features bars on the windows, lamps that look like police flashlights, barbed wire, fingerprints on the bills, wait staff in striped uniforms, and sections of the Russian Penal Code as decorations.

3. In the April 25, 1989, game where Pittsburgh's Mario Lemieux tied the NHL record for most goals in a single playoff game, with five, he also tied the record for most points in a single playoff game, with eight.

4. Agitating center Matt Cooke played what many considered to be a "dirty" brand of hockey and was always looking to stir things up on the ice. Over the course of his career, he was suspended by the NHL for spearing, boarding, elbowing, hits to the head, hits from behind, and knee-on-knee contact.

5. Penguins center Jordan Staal is one of four brothers who

all played in the NHL. They include defenseman Marc Staal and forwards Eric Staal and Jared Staal. Jordan, Eric, and Jared actually played on a forward line together at one point, while with the Carolina Hurricanes.

6. Penguins center Sidney Crosby has impeccable leadership qualifications. Not only is he the youngest player in NHL history to captain his team to a Stanley Cup championship, but he is also the only player in the "Triple Gold Club" (winner of a Stanley Cup, Olympic gold medal, and World Championship gold medal) to be captain of all three winning squads.

7. Maxime Talbot was a well-known figure in the Pittsburgh community. He once appeared on a box of City of Champions Crunch cereal, which displayed Talbot on one side and wide receiver Hines Ward of the Pittsburgh Steelers on the opposite side.

8. Before starring at center for the Penguins, John Cullen enjoyed an interesting time at Boston University. Cullen excelled on the ice, becoming the university's all-time leading scorer. He also dated Carolyn Bessette, who later wound up marrying John F. Kennedy Jr.

9. On March 30, 2013, Pens leader Sidney Crosby took a slap shot from ex-teammate Brooks Orpik directly in the mouth during a game against the New York Islanders. Crosby lost several teeth, suffered a broken jaw, and required major reconstructive surgery. He missed the end of the regular season but did return for the playoffs.

10. Former Pens center Dan Quinn loved golf enough to make a career of it post hockey. He played on the Celebrity Tour, won several tournaments, and has caddied for golf legends, John Daly and Ernie Els.

CHAPTER 11:

THE WINGERS TAKE FLIGHT

QUIZ TIME!

1. Which winger was the first player born and trained in Pittsburgh to take the ice for an NHL game as a member of the Penguins?

    a. Ryan Malone

    b. Joe Mullen

    c. Lowell McDonald

    d. Bryan Rust

2. Penguins winger Randy Cunneyworth once engaged in four separate fights during a line brawl against the Quebec Nordiques.

    a. True

    b. False

3. What type of injury ended winger Pascal Dupuis's playing career with the Penguins?

    a. Blood clots

    b. Concussions

c. Leukemia

d. Loss of vision

4. On May 4, 2000, workhorse winger Jaromir Jagr set the NHL record for most ice time by a forward in a single playoff game. The Penguins lost to the Flyers 2-1 in five overtimes. How long did Jagr spend on the ice?

a. 35 minutes, 22 seconds

b. 41 minutes, 56 seconds

c. 48 minutes, 12 seconds

d. 59 minutes, 8 seconds

5. Promising Penguins winger Wayne Bianchin suffered a broken neck in the offseason after his rookie year. What activity was he participating in when the injury occurred?

a. Horseback riding

b. Weight training

c. Bodysurfing

d. Motorcycle racing

6. Which Penguin winger scored a Stanley Cup-clinching goal against his former team, the Nashville Predators, in 2017?

a. James Neal

b. Patric Hornqvist

c. Carl Hagelin

d. Alexei Kovalev

7. On February 9, 2007, left winger Ryan Malone scored a hat trick by recording a goal within the first minute of each period.

a. True

b. False

8. When the 1991-92 season concluded, only three NHL players had ever outscored the great Wayne Gretzky in a season. Two of them were Penguins. Which two?

a. Mario Lemieux and Jaromir Jagr

b. Mario Lemieux and Kevin Stevens

c. Mark Recchi and Joe Mullen

d. Joe Mullen and Kevin Stevens

9. In 2017, Penguins winger Jake Guentzel tied the NHL record for most points by a rookie in one playoff season. How many points did he score?

a. 15

b. 17

c. 19

d. 21

10. Which Penguins winger, at 37, was the oldest NHL player to score a game-winning goal in a playoff Game 7 to clinch a series victory?

a. Chris Kunitz

b. Jaromir Jagr

c. Rick Kehoe

d. Mark Recchi

11. Pittsburgh right winger Craig Adams was the first and only NHL player born in which country?

a. Haiti

b. Lebanon

c. Nigeria

d. Brunei

12. Penguins winger Bob Errey is a cousin of Indy Car Racing champion Tom Geoghegan.

a. True

b. False

13. Patric Hornqvist set the Penguins record for the fastest natural hat trick in a 6-3 win against the Colorado Avalanche. How long did it take him to score those three goals?

a. 1 minute, 19 seconds

b. 1 minute, 36 seconds

c. 2 minutes, 5 seconds

d. 2 minutes, 47 seconds

14. Pittsburgh's Jaromir Jagr holds one important NHL record involving the number 135. What record does the 135 represent for him?

a. Most times representing his country in international competition

b. Most game-winning goals in a career

c. Most shots on the net in the Stanley Cup Finals in a career

d. Most "first star" awards at the end of a game in a career

15. Which Penguin was the starting right winger in the 40th NHL All-Star Game?

a. Jaromir Jagr

b. Jean Pronovost

c. Rob Brown

d. Phil Kessel

16. Phil Kessel returned to hockey from testicular cancer and began an "Iron Man Streak" of over 500 consecutive NHL games played. He is one of only four current players to actively be on such a streak.

a. True

b. False

17. Pens forward Kevin Stevens once recorded over 50 goals and 200 penalty minutes in a single season. Only three other NHL players have done so. Who does not share this achievement with Stevens?

a. Keith Tkachuk

b. Cam Neely

c. Gary Roberts

d. Brendan Shanahan

18. Which position has former winger Rick Kehoe not held with the Penguins after retiring from his playing career?

a. Director of Pro Scouting

b. Assistant Coach

c. Head Coach

d. General Manager

19. Phil Bourque, who played left wing for the Penguins, wrote a book about his time with the team. What was the book's title?

a. *Mario and Me: Our Quest for the Cup*

b. *Scandalous Tales from a Hockey Hotbed*

c. *If These Walls Could Talk: Pittsburgh Penguins*

d. *He Shoots…Nah, He Passes the Puck to Jagr*

20. Penguins right winger Peter Lee was born in the United Kingdom, raised in Canada, played hockey in the United States, and is a member of the German Ice Hockey Hall of Fame.

a. True

b. False

QUIZ ANSWERS

1. A – Ryan Malone

2. B – False

3. A – Blood clots

4. D – 59 minutes, 8 seconds

5. C – Bodysurfing

6. B – Patric Hornqvist

7. A – True

8. B – Mario Lemieux and Kevin Stevens

9. D – 21

10. A – Chris Kunitz

11. D – Brunei

12. A – True

13. D – 2 minutes, 47 seconds

14. B – Most game-winning goals in a career

15. C – Rob Brown

16. A – True

17. B – Cam Neely

18. D – General Manager

19. C – *If These Walls Could Talk: Pittsburgh Penguins*

20. A – True

DID YOU KNOW?

1. Star Pittsburgh winger Rick Kehoe played hockey cleanly and respectfully. Over his lengthy career, Kehoe averaged less than ten penalty minutes per season and won the Lady Byng Trophy for sportsmanship in 1981.

2. Mark Recchi, who hails from Kamloops, British Columbia, won Stanley Cups with Pittsburgh, Carolina, and Boston, was named Kamloops Male Athlete of the 20th Century, and was honored with a street called "Mark Recchi Way" in his hometown.

3. Penguins icon Jaromir Jagr holds many records, including most assists in a single season and in a career by a right winger, and most points in a single season and in a career by a right winger.

4. Winger Aleksey Morozov did not have the long-term impact of Mario Lemieux in Pittsburgh, but he did match Lemieux's immediate impact. Both players scored on their very first shot, during their very first shift, in their very first game for Pittsburgh.

5. In 1993, Pens winger Kevin Stevens hit New York Islander Rich Pilon so hard that Stevens knocked himself out and fell face-first onto the ice, breaking enough bones in his face that major reconstructive surgery was necessary. The surgeons peeled the skin back from his face, used metal plates to reconnect the bones, and sewed him up with over 100 stitches.

6. At the University of Minnesota, two future Penguins teammates shared an interesting connection. Winger Phil Kessel played for the Golden Gophers hockey team while Jake Guentzel's father, Mike, was the associate head coach. Jake was a stick boy and helped Kessel (among others) with his equipment.

7. Pens winger Craig Adams really knows how to use his brain. Not only did he spend four years at Harvard, but he also became a successful financial advisor in retirement and has agreed to donate his brain to scientists after his death so that they can study the effects of repeated head trauma.

8. Phil Kessel won back-to-back Stanley Cups with the Penguins. On his first day with the Cup, he brought it to his hometown and to SickKids Hospital to share it with patients there. On his second day with the Cup, he famously filled it with hot dogs to eat and posted pictures of this celebration on social media. This allowed Kessel to get the last laugh after a reporter had made fun of him for snacking on hot dogs and questioned his playing weight.

9. Model of consistency Jaromir Jagr is tied for the NHL record for most consecutive 30 (or more) goal seasons, with 15. Ten of those seasons came with Pittsburgh before he began playing for the Washington Capitals. Current Capitals star Alex Ovechkin is tied for this record as well, and could potentially break it next year.

10. Pittsburgh winger Val Fonteyne played a remarkably

clean brand of hockey. During 13 seasons and over 800 NHL games, Fonteyne was assessed only 26 total penalty minutes. He went unpenalized five complete seasons (including three consecutively), and had a single fight throughout his whole career. During his time with the Oilers in the WHA, Fonteyne recorded another 149 games with only 4 penalty minutes.

CHAPTER 12:

COACHES, GMS, & OWNERS

QUIZ TIME!

1. Who served as the Penguins' first general manager?

    a. Scotty Bowman

    b. Punch Imlach

    c. Al Arbour

    d. Jack Riley

2. The Penguins boast more head coaches who have been elected to the Hall of Fame than any other NHL franchise.

    a. True

    b. False

3. The Penguins' first head coach, George Sullivan, lasted for how long in that position with the franchise?

    a. 38 days

    b. 1 season

    c. 2 seasons

    d. 10 seasons

4. Which former Pittsburgh Penguin player is now a part owner of the franchise, after converting $32.5 million in salary owed into equity instead?

    a. Jaromir Jagr
    b. Tom Barrasso
    c. Mario Lemieux
    d. Jean Pronovost

5. Who has owned the Pittsburgh Penguins for the longest amount of time?

    a. Howard Baldwin, Morris Belzberg, and Thomas Ruta
    b. Mario Lemieux and Ron Burkle
    c. Edward DeBartolo
    d. Al Savill and Otto Frenzel

6. The Penguins stitched the words "A Great Day for Hockey" onto the back neckline of their 2019 Stadium Series jerseys as a tribute to which Penguins coach?

    a. Bob Johnson
    b. Mike Sullivan
    c. Dan Bylsma
    d. Kevin Constantine

7. The Penguins Hall of Fame has inducted more owners and GMs than coaches, goalies, and left wingers combined.

    a. True
    b. False

8. When Penguins owner Edward J. DeBartolo passed away, a team award was created in his memory. What does the award recognize?

a. Leadership

b. Commitment to Excellence

c. Fair Play

d. Community Service

9. Which coach led the Penguins to their second Stanley Cup championship?

   a. Scotty Bowman

   b. Bob Johnson

   c. Dan Bylsma

   d. Kevin Constantine

10. How many of the Penguins 22 head coaches have spent their entire NHL coaching career with Pittsburgh?

    a. 0

    b. 1

    c. 8

    d. 17

11. Which of the following jobs has Eddie Olczyk not held with the Penguins franchise?

    a. Player

    b. Coach

    c. General Manager

    d. Broadcaster

12. Penguins coach and general manager Red Kelly received the Order of Canada; the second-highest honor the country can bestow.

    a. True

    b. False

13. Which player was not signed as a free agent by general manager Craig Patrick in 2005, when the Penguins reloaded after drafting Sidney Crosby?

   a. Jocelyn Thibault
   b. John LeClair
   c. Ziggy Palffy
   d. Sergei Gonchar

14. Which Penguins coach has a team award named after him, given to a player for "his performance on the ice, his character and total dedication to his teammates for the success of the team"?

   a. Scotty Bowman
   b. Mike Sullivan
   c. Bob Johnson
   d. Dan Bylsma

15. Why did Penguins coach Bob Johnson not coach the team in 1992 after leading them to a Stanley Cup victory in 1991?

   a. He retired after the 1991 season.
   b. He was fired for insubordination during the offseason.
   c. He took a job coaching the United States national team.
   d. He passed away due to cancer.

16. Penguins general manager Jim Rutherford played goalie for the team during his NHL playing career.

   a. True
   b. False

17. When the Penguins struggled financially in 2007 and could not convince the city of Pittsburgh to build a new arena, where did ownership consider relocating the franchise?

    a. Quebec City
    b. Kansas City
    c. Houston
    d. Hamilton

18. Which former Penguins players are currently working as assistant coaches with the team?

    a. Kevin Stevens and Paul Coffey
    b. Bill Guerin and Zarley Zalapski
    c. Mark Recchi and Sergei Gonchar
    d. John Cullen and Ulf Samuelsson

19. Which Penguins coach is the only one to have won the Jack Adams Award as the league's top coach, while behind the bench for Pittsburgh?

    a. Scotty Bowman
    b. Gene Ubriaco
    c. Bob Johnson
    d. Dan Bylsma

20. Mario Lemieux and Sidney Crosby have both stated their intention for Lemieux to pass on ownership of the franchise to Crosby once his playing days are over.

    a. True
    b. False

QUIZ ANSWERS

1. D – Jack Riley

2. B – False

3. C – 2 seasons

4. C – Mario Lemieux

5. B – Mario Lemieux and Ronald Burkle

6. A – Bob Johnson

7. A – True

8. D – Community Service

9. B – Bob Johnson

10. C – 8

11. C – General Manager

12. A – True

13. A – Jocelyn Thibault

14. C – Bob Johnson

15. D – He passed away due to cancer.

16. A – True

17. B – Kansas City

18. C – Mark Recchi and Sergei Gonchar

19. D – Dan Bylsma

20. B – False

DID YOU KNOW?

1. Penguins coach and general manager Red Kelly was also a member of parliament in the Canadian House of Commons. He represented the Liberal Party and served two terms before declining to seek re-election so he could spend more time with his family.

2. Current Penguins owner Ronald Burkle has appeared on Forbes magazine's "The Richest People on the Planet" list. His net worth is estimated at approximately $2 billion.

3. Penguins owners Howard Baldwin and Morris Belzberg spent freely during the 1990s to help the Penguins continue to win, but they asked many players to defer their salaries. When these (and other) payments came due, the owners had to file for bankruptcy in 1998.

4. After Pittsburgh's bankruptcy scare in the 1970s, general manager Baz Bastien made a series of trades for established veteran players who might help draw fans to the arena but gave up many good draft picks in doing so, which led to poor records for the team in the early 1980s.

5. In 2000, an unusual situation occurred when team owner Mario Lemieux decided to return to the league from retirement. It was extremely rare for someone to own and play for a team at the same time, but Lemieux did help the Penguins make the playoffs that season.

6. Former Penguins coach Ivan Hlinka has an international,

under-18 hockey tournament named after him. Hlinka was a major figure in Czech hockey but was killed in a car accident in 2004, at age 54.

7. General manager Craig Patrick had an incredible offseason in 1990. He loaded up the Penguins for future Stanley Cups by adding Bryan Trottier in free agency, Jaromir Jagr in the NHL Draft, and Joe Mullen, Ron Francis, Ulf Samuelsson, and Larry Murphy in trades. All would go on to play significant roles in Pittsburgh's success on the ice.

8. For a short time, during June-July 1975, the Penguins were owned by the NHL itself after the former owners, Peter Block, Thayer Potter, Elmore Keener, and Peter Burchfield, ran into financial difficulty. This was not an ideal situation, so the league quickly found a buyer in the trio of Al Savill, Otto Frenzel, and Wren Blair.

9. Twice, Pittsburgh general managers have been awarded the NHL General Manager of the Year Trophy. Ray Shero won it in 2013, and Jim Rutherford claimed the prize in 2016.

10. The Penguins' very first coach, Red Sullivan, was succeeded by a coach with the same nickname, Red Kelly. Their current coach, Mike Sullivan, succeeded a coach with the same first name, Mike Johnston.

CHAPTER 13:

THE AWARDS SECTION

QUIZ TIME!

1. Which Penguin has won the most Hart Trophies as league MVP while playing for Pittsburgh?

   a. Sidney Crosby

   b. Jaromir Jagr

   c. Evgeni Malkin

   d. Mario Lemieux

2. The first Penguin to win any major award given out by the NHL was franchise center Mario Lemieux.

   a. True

   b. False

3. During which season did the Penguins win their first Presidents' Trophy for leading the NHL in points?

   a. 1969-70

   b. 1976-77

   c. 1985-86

   d. 1992-93

4. Who was the first Penguin to win the Lester Patrick Trophy for outstanding service to hockey in the United States?

    a. Craig Patrick
    b. Joe Mullen
    c. Herb Brooks
    d. Ross Lonsberry

5. How many goals did Sidney Crosby score in 2009-10 to take home the Maurice "Rocket" Richard Trophy for most goals in the NHL?

    a. 51
    b. 55
    c. 63
    d. 74

6. Which two Penguins were selected to play together in the 2008 NHL YoungStars game?

    a. Bryan Rust and Conor Sheary
    b. Kris Letang and Tyler Kennedy
    c. Evgeni Malkin and James Neal
    d. Hal Gill and Tyler Wright

7. Evgeni Malkin has won more Kharlamov Trophies (for best Russian player in the NHL) than Jaromir Jagr.

    a. True
    b. False

8. Which Pittsburgh forward won both the Art Ross and Conn Smythe Trophies during the Penguins' run to the Stanley Cup in the 2008-09 season?

a. Sidney Crosby

b. Jordan Staal

c. Bill Guerin

d. Evgeni Malkin

9. Only one Penguin has ever won the Frank J. Selke Trophy as the NHL's best defensive forward. Who was it?

a. Robert Lang

b. Jordan Staal

c. Ron Francis

d. Bob Errey

10. Which two players have won back-to-back Conn Smythe Trophies for Pittsburgh as Stanley Cup Finals MVP?

a. Mario Lemieux and Evgeni Malkin

b. Mario Lemieux and Sidney Crosby

c. Jaromir Jagr and Evgeni Malkin

d. Jaromir Jagr and Sidney Crosby

11. The Lady Byng Memorial Trophy for sportsmanship, gentlemanly conduct, and playing ability has been won by which two Penguins in franchise history?

a. Rick Kehoe and Ron Francis

b. Jean Pronovost and Mario Lemieux

c. Earl Ingarfield and Phil Kessel

d. John Cullen and Joe Mullen

12. Sidney Crosby won the Calder Trophy as rookie of the year over competition that included both teammate Evgeni Malkin and Capitals winger Alexander Ovechkin.

a. True

b. False

13. Which of the following Penguins players won the Calder Memorial Trophy as the league's top rookie?

    a. Sidney Crosby

    b. Jaromir Jagr

    c. Marc-Andre Fleury

    d. Evgeni Malkin

14. How many times did team captain Mario Lemieux win the Penguins' Player's Player Award, for exemplifying leadership and teamwork?

    a. 2

    b. 5

    c. 8

    d. 11

15. Sidney Crosby is the only Penguin to win the Maurice "Rocket" Richard Trophy as the NHL's leading goal scorer. In 2010, he shared the trophy in a tie with which other NHL player?

    a. Jarome Iginla

    b. Alexander Ovechkin

    c. Daniel Alfredsson

    d. Steven Stamkos

16. Despite being an expansion team 50 years after the NHL began, the Pittsburgh Penguins boast more Art Ross Trophy winners than any other franchise.

a. True

b. False

17. Penguins star Mario Lemieux won the 1993 Art Ross Trophy as the NHL's top scorer with 160 points despite missing 24 games due to what ailment?

    a. Sprained MCL
    b. Broken clavicle
    c. Hodgkin's lymphoma
    d. Diabetes

18. Which trophy did center Evgeni Malkin not win after the conclusion of the 2011-12 NHL season?

    a. Lady Byng Trophy
    b. Art Ross Trophy
    c. Hart Memorial Trophy
    d. Lester B. Pearson Award

19. Two players have won back-to-back awards as Penguins Defensive Player of the Year. Which two were they?

    a. Jordan Staal and Paul Martin
    b. Matt Niskanen and Kris Letang
    c. Kris Letang and Brooks Orpik
    d. Marc-Andre Fleury and Matt Murray

20. Although the Penguins have only retired two numbers, there are 16 members of the "Penguins' Ring of Honor."

    a. True
    b. False

QUIZ ANSWERS

1. D – Mario Lemieux

2. B – False

3. D – 1992-93

4. B – Joe Mullen

5. A – 51

6. B – Kris Letang and Tyler Kennedy

7. A – True

8. D – Evgeni Malkin

9. C – Ron Francis

10. B – Mario Lemieux and Sidney Crosby

11. A – Rick Kehoe and Ron Francis

12. B – False

13. D – Evgeni Malkin

14. A – 2

15. D – Steven Stamkos

16. A – True

17. C – Hodgkin's lymphoma

18. A – Lady Byng Trophy

19. C – Kris Letang and Brooks Orpik

20. A – True

DID YOU KNOW?

1. The Bill Masterton Trophy, for perseverance, sportsmanship, and dedication to hockey, has been won by two Penguins, twenty years apart. Lowell McDonald was awarded the trophy in 1973, and Mario Lemieux received it in 1993.

2. The Penguins have twice won back-to-back Stanley Cup championships. They first accomplished this is 1991 and 1992, then again in 2016 and 2017. Their wins in 2016 and 2017 make them the only club to win back-to-back titles during the NHL's salary cap era.

3. Offense has always been the Penguins' calling card. Only one Pittsburgh defender has ever won the James Norris Trophy (Randy Carlyle, in 1981). Since that time, a Penguin has won the Art Ross Trophy as the NHL's leading scorer fifteen times.

4. Twelve players who skated with Pittsburgh have been elected to the Hockey Hall of Fame. Ten of the twelve were born in Canada, but American Joe Mullen and Russian Sergei Zubov were also selected for enshrinement.

5. Mario Lemieux won four Lester B. Pearson/Ted Lindsay Awards as the NHL's most outstanding player, but never won in consecutive years. Although Jaromir Jagr and Sidney Crosby have won the award fewer times, both won it in back-to-back seasons.

6. Pittsburgh's five Stanley Cup championships ties them with the Edmonton Oilers for most title wins by a team that was not founded in the NHL's Original Six era.

7. Defenseman Kris Letang not only won the Emile Bouchard Trophy and Kevin Lowe Trophy (as the AHL's best defenseman and best defensive defenseman, respectively) but also took home an unusual award: The Paul Dumont Trophy, awarded to the player with the best personality.

8. Superstar Mario Lemieux was so revered around the league that when he announced his initial retirement in 1997 due to health issues and frustration with officiating, the customary three-year delay was waived, and he was inducted into the Hockey Hall of Fame immediately.

9. The Lester Patrick Trophy is awarded each year for outstanding service to hockey in the United States. From 2000 to 2002, four Penguins won the trophy. Mario Lemieux and Craig Patrick shared it in 2000, Scotty Bowman got it in 2001, and Herb Brooks was a recipient in 2002.

10. In addition to star players like Mario Lemieux and Paul Coffey, the Penguins Hall of Fame also includes two locker room attendants (Frank Sciulli and Anthony Caggiano) and an organist (Vince Lascheid).

CONCLUSION

There you have it, an amazing collection of Penguins trivia, information, and statistics at your fingertips! Regardless of how you fared on the quizzes, we hope that you found this book entertaining, enlightening, and educational.

Ideally, you knew many of these details, but also learned a good deal more about the history of the Pittsburgh Penguins, their players, coaches, management, and some of the quirky stories surrounding the team. If you got a little peek into the colorful details that make being a fan so much more enjoyable, then mission accomplished!

The good news is the trivia doesn't have to stop there! Spread the word. Challenge your fellow Penguins fans to see if they can do any better. Share some of the stories with the next generation to help them become Pittsburgh supporters too.

If you are a big enough Penguins fan, consider creating your own quiz with some of the details you know that weren't presented here, and then test your friends to see if they can match your knowledge.

The Pittsburgh Penguins are a storied franchise. They have a long history with multiple periods of success (and a few that were less than successful). They've had glorious superstars, iconic moments, hilarious tales...but most of all they have wonderful, passionate fans. Thank you for being one of them.

Made in the USA
Las Vegas, NV
19 December 2024

14718764R00077